T0087425

The Inner Enemies of
Democracy

Tzvetan Todorov

THE INNER ENEMIES OF DEMOCRACY

Translated by Andrew Brown

polity

First published in French as *Les ennemis intimes de la démocratie*
© Editions Robert Laffont/Versilio, 2012

This English edition © Polity Press, 2014

Polity Press
65 Bridge Street
Cambridge CB2 1UR, UK

Polity Press
350 Main Street
Malden, MA 02148, USA

ISBN-13: 978-0-7456-8574-8

A catalogue record for this book is available from the British Library.

Library of Congress Cataloging-in-Publication Data
Todorov, Tzvetan, 1939-
  [Ennemis intimes de la démocratie. English]
  The inner enemies of democracy / Tzvetan Todorov.
    pages cm
  ISBN 978-0-7456-8574-8 (hardback) -- ISBN 0-7456-8574-9 (hardback)
1. Democracy. 2. World politics. I. Title.
  JC423.T6213 2014
  321.8--dc23
                                                          2014012440

Typeset in 11 on 13 Sabon by Servis Filmsetting Ltd, Stockport, Cheshire
Printed and bound in the United Kingdom by T.J. International Ltd, Padstow, Cornwall

The publisher has used its best endeavours to ensure that the URLs for external websites referred to in this book are correct and active at the time of going to press. However, the publisher has no responsibility for the websites and can make no guarantee that a site will remain live or that the content is or will remain appropriate.

Every effort has been made to trace all copyright holders, but if any have been inadvertently overlooked the publisher will be pleased to include any necessary credits in any subsequent reprint or edition.

For further information on Polity, visit our website: politybooks.com

Contents

1

Democracy and its Discontents

The paradoxes of freedom

The question of freedom entered my life early on. Until the age of twenty-four, I lived in a totalitarian country, Communist Bulgaria. The main thing everyone around me complained about was the shortages – the difficulty of getting hold of not just basic commodities but those little 'extras' that brighten up life, such as food, clothing, toiletries and furnishings. But the lack of freedom still came next on the list of gripes. The country's leaders exercised control over countless activities through a whole range of different organizations, through occupation, neighbourhood and age group, as well as through the party apparatus, the police force and the political police known as 'State Security'. Our whole life was monitored, and the slightest deviation from the party line risked being denounced. This obviously included all the areas that could be related to the political principles laid down, from literature and the human sciences to public institutions. But it also included more neutral aspects of life, aspects that it would be difficult to imagine, in other circumstances, as having any ideological meaning at all: the choice of a place of residence or of a profession, and even something as seemingly frivolous as your preference for a particular garment. Wearing a

1

miniskirt, or trousers that were too tight (or too loose), was severely punished. It could lead you, first, to the police station where you were given a couple of slaps in the face; for a subsequent offence, you could end up in a 're-education' camp, and you were never sure you would get out alive.

We suffered from this lack of freedom to a degree that depended on how much we needed it. I was a curious young man, living in the capital, studying literature, preparing myself for an intellectual profession, teaching or writing. The word 'freedom' was, of course, legitimate and even highly valued, but like the other ingredients of official propaganda, it was used to hide – or to fill in for – an absence: for lack of the real thing, we had the word. Those who wanted to participate in public life without becoming slaves of dogma were asked to practise a variant of the 'forgotten art of writing' of which Leo Strauss speaks, the language of Aesop: do not *say* a thing but *suggest* it – a subtle game in which you, too, could end up being the loser. For my part, I was sensitive to the lack of freedom of expression, a lack which eroded the very freedom of thought on which it was based. I had witnessed – in silence – the public humiliation of several people whose behaviour had been found to deviate too much from the model imposed, and I hoped to spare myself such sessions of 'critique' without betraying my convictions.

During the last year I spent in Bulgaria before leaving, fresh out of college, I took my first tentative steps in public life by writing for newspapers. I was especially proud when I felt I had managed to get round the all-pervasive censorship. On the occasion of a national holiday, they had asked me to prepare a double-page spread in a newspaper. I chose to mention some dead heroes of the anti-fascist resistance who had fought against tyranny: these were characters of undeniable virtue. My stratagem consisted of talking about the present under cover of evoking the past, so as to remind everyone that freedom has to be fought for. This was indeed the title I had chosen for these pages: 'For freedom!' Many people, I remember, noticed this publication and, understanding the allusion to the present, praised me for my ingenuity . . . Such were the paltry victories which a young Bulgarian author could boast of, in those days. Freedom, in any case, was the value that was most dear to me.

I will now leap forward forty-eight years, to the Europe of today. And here, with a mixture of puzzlement and anxiety, I discover that the word 'freedom' is still not associated with practices that I can approve of. In 2011, the term seems to have become a brand name for political parties of the extreme right, nationalist and xenophobic in character: the Party for Freedom in the Netherlands, headed by Geert Wilders, or the Austrian Freedom Party, led until his death by Jörg Haider. The Northern League, under Umberto Bossi, has candidates at Italian elections standing as representatives of the League of the People of Freedom, joining Berlusconi's People of Freedom. The wave of anti-Muslim and anti-African reaction in Germany that followed the success of a book by Thilo Sarrazin has led to the creation of a party based on his ideas, called Die Freiheit ('Freedom'), with the programme of 'fighting against the rampant Islamization of Europe'. In Ukraine since 1995 there has been a nationalist party called Svoboda ('Freedom'), which campaigns against foreign, Russian or Western influences and against the presence of foreigners; its slogan is 'Ukraine for the Ukrainians'. The questionable use of the word 'freedom' is not entirely new: in the late nineteenth century the newspaper of French anti-Semitism, edited by Édouard Drumont, was called *La libre parole* (*Free Speech*).

I had thought at first that freedom was a fundamental value of democracy; I have since realized that a certain use of freedom can be a danger to democracy.

Could this be a sign that, today, the threats to it come, not from the outside, from those who openly present themselves as its enemies, but from within, from the ideologies, movements or actions which claim to defend democratic values? Or could it be a sign that the values in question are not always good ones?

External and internal enemies

The major political event of the twentieth century in the Northern hemisphere was the clash between democracies and totalitarian regimes, with the latter claiming that they intended to correct the defects of the former. This conflict was responsible for World War II, some sixty million deaths and an infinite amount of suffering: it ended with the victory of democracy. Nazism was defeated in 1945, and the collapse of Communism occurred in November 1989: the event that symbolized the denouement was the fall of the Berlin Wall. Any resurrection of the totalitarian threat in the near future is inconceivable. It is true that several countries around the world continue to claim that they are Communist in ideology; however, they are no longer perceived as a threat, but as anachronisms that cannot survive for long. The only one among them which is a great power, China, no longer corresponds to the 'ideal type' of the totalitarian regime. Instead, China appears to observers as a baroque hybrid, made up of Communist rhetoric, a repressive centralized administration, and a market economy that allows and even encourages an opening to the outside world and the personal enrichment of individuals, things that would have been inconceivable under Soviet or Maoist Communism. It is hard to imagine, in the foreseeable future, any Chinese military aggression against Western democracies. The end of the Cold War has put an end to the Communist threat.

At the turn of the century, due to the combined activities of various influential political commentators and the attack of September 11, 2001, against the United States, it was claimed that a new enemy had taken the place of the old foe. This new enemy was an Islamic fundamentalism that called for a holy war against all democracies, the United States first and foremost. The destruction of the Twin Towers in New York by suicide pilots resulted in the deaths of 3,000 people, had a huge and widespread impact, and revealed a real danger. But to compare it to the danger presented by the Soviet empire would be exaggerated. Even though Islamic fundamentalism is a force to be reckoned with in Muslim-majority countries, the threat posed by its international version (known as al-Qaeda) to Western countries is incommensurate with that embodied by the Communist countries: it is a threat that requires police vigilance rather than the intervention of a powerful army. The violence that it incarnates revives memories of the Red Army Faction in Germany and the Red Brigades in Italy, rather than of Stalin's Red Army.

If terrorist acts of this nature have left a lasting mark on democratic societies, this is less because of the damage they have inflicted on these societies than because of the dramatic reactions they have aroused. The United States reacted to this cunning provocation like a bull charging at a red rag. What proportion can be established between the one-off attack on the Twin Towers of New York and the wars in Afghanistan and Iraq, which have lasted for years, have claimed hundreds of thousands of victims, cost billions of dollars and undermined for a long time to come the reputation (and, indirectly, the safety) of the United States in the region? In addition, this policy has inflicted damage even *within* the country, a damage that has had a knock-on effect on the United States' European allies: these include the legal acceptance of torture, discrimination against minorities and restrictions on civil liberties.

Islamic terrorism (or jihadism) is not a credible candidate for the role of enemy that was formerly held by Moscow. No model of society other than the democratic regime has as yet come forward as its rival; on the contrary, we see a desire for democracy arising almost anywhere where it was previously absent. This does not mean that democracies no longer bother to protect themselves with arms: the world's population has not been suddenly replaced by a choir of angels, and there are still many reasons for hostility or aggression between peoples; but there is no longer any global enemy or planetary rival. However, democracy secretes within itself the very forces that threaten it, and the novelty of our time is that these forces are superior to those attacking it from outside. Combating and neutralizing them is all the more difficult because they claim to be imbued with the democratic spirit, and thus have every appearance of legitimacy.

In itself there is nothing paradoxical about such a situation in which evil arises from good: there are many well-known examples. In the twentieth century, we learned that man has become a threat to his own survival. Thanks to the dazzling, rapid advances in science, he has penetrated some of the secrets of matter and is now able to transform it; but this also means he is threatened by nuclear explosions as well as by global warming, by the greenhouse effect as well as by the mutation of species that results from genetic manipulation. Contrary to what our ancestors thought in the eighteenth and nineteenth centuries, we have become convinced that, as well as being a purveyor of hope, science can be a danger to our very survival. The same goes for technological innovations that reduce our physical efforts, but often deplete the life of the mind: it all depends on the use we make of them.

We are proud of the principle of equality of rights between individuals and between peoples; at the same time, we can see that, if all the inhabitants of the earth based their consumption of goods on that of Western populations, our planet would soon run out of resources. We say out loud and clear that every human being has the same right to life, so we welcome the progress of preventive medicine that reduces child mortality, yet we know that the unlimited growth of the world population would be a catastrophe.

These paradoxical situations are very familiar to us. The way that democracy creates its own enemies is a little less familiar.

Democracy threatened by its own hubris

A democratic regime is defined by a set of features that combine together to form a complex arrangement in which these features limit and balance each other: although they do not come into direct contradiction with each other, they have different sources and purposes. If this balance is broken, alarm bells should start to ring.

Democracy is first, in its etymological sense, a regime in which power belongs to the people. In practice, the entire population chooses its representatives, who, in a sovereign way, make the laws and govern the country for a period of time determined in advance. Democracy is distinguished from traditional societies, which claim to submit to principles handed down from their ancestors, and from absolute monarchies under a king ruling by divine right, where the succession of leaders depends on belonging to the same family. The people, in a democracy, do not comprise a 'natural' substance. They are different not only quantitatively but qualitatively from the family, clan and tribe (where what matters is kinship), and they are different too from any collective entity defined by the presence of a trait such as race, religion or original language. The people are comprised of all those who were born on the same soil, plus those who have been accepted by them. In a democracy, at least in theory, all citizens have equal rights, all inhabitants are equal in dignity.

Modern democracies are said to be liberal when a second fundamental principle is added: the freedom of individuals. The people remain sovereign, as any other choice would involve submitting them to an external force, but their power is limited: it must come to an end at the borders of individual persons who are masters in their own home. One part of their lives falls within the scope of the public power, while another is independent: personal fulfilment has become a legitimate purpose of individual existence. So we cannot regulate life in society in the name of a single principle: the welfare of the community does not coincide with that of the individual. The relationship that develops between the two forms of autonomy, the sovereignty of the people and the freedom of the individual, is that of a mutual limitation: individuals must not impose their will on the community, which in turn should not interfere in the private affairs of its citizens.

Democracies also rest on a certain conception of political action. They try, again, to avoid two extremes. On the one hand, unlike theocracies and totalitarian regimes, they do not promise they can give salvation to their populations, nor do they prescribe the path that will lead to salvation. Building heaven on earth is not part of their programme, and the imperfection of all social order is considered to be an irreducible given. But, on the other hand, democracies are not to be confused with traditionalist and conservative regimes, where it is believed that no rule imposed by tradition should ever be questioned. Democracies reject the fatalistic attitude of resignation. This intermediate position allows different interpretations, but we can say that any democracy implies the idea of a possible improvement of the social order, a development through the efforts of the collective will. The word 'progress' is viewed with suspicion nowadays, but the idea behind it is inherent in the democratic project. And the result is clear: the inhabitants of democratic countries, although they are often dissatisfied with their condition, live in a more just world than those of other countries. They are protected by law; there is solidarity between members of the society, which benefits the old, the sick, the unemployed and the destitute; they can appeal to the principles of equality and liberty, or even to a spirit of fraternity.

Democracy is characterized not only by the mode of institution of its power, or by the goal of its actions, but also by the manner in which power is exercised. The key word here is *pluralism*, because it is deemed that all powers, however legitimate, should not be handled by the same people or concentrated in the same institutions. It is essential that the judiciary should not be subject to political power (which combines the executive and legislative), but that it should be able to pass judgement independently. The same goes for media power, the latest form of power on the scene, which must not be placed exclusively at the service of the government but must itself remain plural. The economy, dependent on private property, retains its autonomy from political power, which, in turn, does not become a mere instrument in the service of the economic interests of a few tycoons. The will of the people also comes up against a boundary of a different order: to prevent it from being affected by a transient emotion or a clever manipulation of public opinion, it must remain consistent with principles defined after careful consideration and enshrined in the constitution of the country, or simply inherited from the wisdom of the peoples.

The dangers inherent in the idea of democracy itself stem from isolating and promoting only one of its ingredients. What links these various dangers is a form of excess. The people, freedom and progress are constituent elements of democracy, but if one of them breaks free from its relations with others, thus escaping any attempt to limit it and erecting itself into a single principle, they become distinct dangers: populism, ultraliberalism and messianism, those inner enemies of democracy.

What the ancient Greeks called hubris, or excess, was considered the worst failing of human action: a desire drunk on itself, a pride persuading the person it fills that, for him, everything is possible. Its opposite was viewed as the political virtue par excellence: moderation, temperance. One of the first to discuss it, Herodotus, recounts in his *History* a case of hubris that led to catastrophic consequences. The Persian king Xerxes wanted to go to war against the Athenians to extend further the boundaries of his kingdom and his power; before making his final decision, he asked his advisors for their opinion. One of them, Artabanus, tried to dissuade him from going to war:

> God is wont to cut short all those things which stand out above the rest. Thus also a numerous army is destroyed by one of few men in some such manner as this, namely when God having become jealous of them casts upon them panic or thundering from heaven, then they are destroyed utterly and not as their worth deserves; for God suffers not any other to have high thoughts save only himself.[1]

The king did not listen to this sage advice; the consequences for himself and his country were indeed disastrous.

Among the ancient Greeks, the gods punish the pride of men who want to take their place and believe they can decide everything; among Christians, the human being is afflicted even before birth by original sin, which severely limits all his aspirations. The people of modern democratic countries do not necessarily believe in gods or in original sin; but there is a brake on their ambitions, namely the very complexity of the social fabric and the democratic regime, the many demands such a system must reconcile and the conflicting interests it must satisfy. The first enemy of democracy is the simplification that reduces the plural to the single and thus opens the way to excess.

To discuss the internal threats to democracy as they arise from its constituent elements – progress, freedom, people – I will in this book draw on my own experience, as I spent the first third of my life in a totalitarian country and the other two thirds in a liberal democracy. Having in the meanwhile become a historian of ideas, I could not help but illustrate my subject by recalling a few stories from the past; but these allusions are brief and are not intended to replace the analyses carried out elsewhere, by myself or others. My presentation is not exhaustive, and I ignore other internal threats to democracy: I mention only what is most familiar to me. I am indebted to various authors cited in the text, but especially to my friend François Flahault, philosopher and social science scholar, whose remarks and writings have given me food for thought for decades. My goal in these pages is not to propose remedies or recipes, but to help people better understand the time and space in which we live.

2

An Ancient Controversy

The main characters

Before getting to the heart of the matter, I would like to mention an episode from the distant past, because I hope it will help to clarify the present.

The story took place about 1,600 years ago, and the initial location of the action was Rome. During the fourth century, Christianity began to gain political power; at the beginning of the century, the Emperor Constantine was converted, and one of his successors, Theodosius, made Christianity the official religion of the empire and banned the pagan rites. Rome became a forum for debate between advocates of different interpretations of Christian dogma. Among them was a self-assured and persuasive preacher named Pelagius, from the British Isles. He must have been born around 350, and arrived in Rome around 380. In his sermons, he criticized the dissolute lifestyle of the wealthy Romans and asked them to take immediate action to ensure their salvation: they must obey Christian precepts, renounce the pleasures of the flesh and give their wealth to the poor. Their destiny was in their own hands, and they were responsible for each of their failings. His teaching impressed young men of good family, who formed around him a circle of disciples. They repented of their sinful past lives, and were drawn to sainthood.

Theological controversies were not the only concern of the Romans. For some time, tribes from the north had been attacking the empire with terrifying force; in 408, led by their leader Alaric, the Visigoths laid siege to the city. They were repulsed, but returned at the end of the following year. Between the two attacks, the Romans began to flee. Among them was Pelagius, accompanied by a few disciples: in 409, he embarked on a journey that would lead first to Carthage, a Roman province in North Africa, then to the nearby town of Hippo, where he asked to meet the Christian bishop, a certain Augustine.

Augustine was born in North Africa and was roughly the same age as Pelagius; and, like him, had gone to Italy, where he converted to Christianity. Augustine returned to his native land a few years later, became a priest, and then, in 395, bishop of Hippo. A prolific author, at home in both classical culture and the new theology, he was involved in numerous controversies with rival Christian thinkers. At the very end of the century, he wrote and published a deeply original book, the *Confessions*, which describes his life and his Christian faith. Pelagius had heard of Augustine in Rome, and he did not agree with all his ideas. He was particularly outraged to find that the bishop lacked confidence in his own strength and preferred to bow to the will of God. Augustine knew nothing of Pelagius' reservations, but perhaps he had heard of his doctrines, which in turn were not to his liking; at all events, he politely turned down the offer of an encounter: the two men never met.

After a year, Pelagius left North Africa and went to Palestine, where many other Roman refugees passionate about matters of faith had gathered. In and around Jerusalem, religious controversy was rife, and Pelagius and his disciples played an active part. A council condemned their interpretation of Christianity in 411, which did not prevent Pelagius publishing several letters and treatises in subsequent years. In 415, a synod cleared him of any accusation of heresy. Augustine was informed and decided to enter the fray. That same year, he wrote an anti-Pelagian treatise, entitled *On Nature and Grace*, and many other texts by him on the subject appeared in subsequent years. The Pelagian controversy would preoccupy him until his death in 430. It was one of the most important in the history of Christianity, and its repercussions are still with us. What was it all about?[1]

Pelagius: will and perfection

For Pelagius, human beings cannot have been given a completely evil nature. Pelagius was fully aware, of course, of what he could see all around him: the fact that the love of money is insatiable and the desire for honours never satisfied; but it would be foolish to reduce men to those evil tendencies. Man is not, or not only, a wolf to man. Moreover, if he were so bad, all hope of improvement would be vain: what could we rely on, how could we even ask for virtues that went against our nature? This initial assumption comes from the Bible: God created man in His image (Genesis 1:27) – and God is good. We also have empirical confirmation: when we perform vile acts, we are aware of doing wrong, we blush, we feel regret or shame. This awareness is common to all human beings, and it is on the side of good; it is a kind of moral tribunal sitting within us, and it does not depend on the doctrines we believe in, as pagans have it just as much as do Christians.

Among the positive dispositions with which men are endowed, one deserves to be distinguished. The God of the Bible enjoyed a freedom of will that enabled him to create the world and mankind out of nothing. If God made man in his image, man, in turn, has a free will. Pelagius finds support for his belief in a biblical text that was often quoted subsequently in similar contexts: we read in the Greek version of Ecclesiasticus (or Sirach) (15:14) that God 'created man and left him in the power of his own decision' (another translation of the original Hebrew says 'in the hand of his deliberation'). And, just as the divine will knows no limits, the human will can overcome all obstacles. It is because we have a will that we can direct our actions and distinguish good from evil. 'We do neither good nor evil without the exercise of our will and always have the freedom to do one of the two' (*To Demetria*, 8.12).[2] A being entirely determined by his nature cannot be subject to moral judgement. The dignity of man comes from his ability to choose, and it is through this deliberative faculty that he is distinguished from the animals.

This undermines the very idea of original sin. If all members of the human race are sinners, whatever they do, simply because they are descended from Adam, this implies that a limit is set to their wills – and, indirectly, to God's will. Pelagius reasoned as follows: if the act we are asked to perform is not within our capabilities, its non-fulfilment cannot be called a sin. You cannot blame someone for not having run a hundred miles in an hour: it is more than a human being can possibly do. If we can describe an act as a sin, we must have been able to do differently, so the act lies within our will. If temptation is overcome, it will be by our own merit; if we fail, it will be through our own fault. 'Sin is due to a fault of will, not of nature' (*To an older friend*, 1.5). If we sin, it is not because we have *inherited* the sin of Adam, it is because we *imitate* the behaviour of our ancestor: this sin is not inborn but acquired.

Even if there were no dogmatic reasons to deny the existence of an insurmountable obstacle to our own improvement, the logic of education should force us to affirm the contrary: the best form of pedagogy lies in highlighting the good tendencies that are innate in us. If we know we are condemned in advance to sin, a great spur to action disappears: we abandon any effort, we accept our destiny, we resign ourselves to the evil we have done. This is precisely what Pelagius criticizes in the doctrine of Augustine, as he read it in the *Confessions*. A criminal could ask us to excuse his crime on the pretext that he has been pressured by original sin! However, if we know that there was nothing inevitable in our action and that we could have done otherwise, we will be encouraged to correct our behaviour.

Man can thus save himself. That does not render divine intervention completely superfluous, but it does lead us to define its place. Once an individual has come into being, he should not expect to receive God's grace to get out of a bad situation; he must rely on his own strength. Grace is essential, but it consists precisely in the fact that, right from the start, God endowed man with freedom. Augustine later summarized the reasoning of the Pelagians in these terms: 'No need, they say, for help from God to fulfil his commandments, because his grace gave us free will.'[3] In short, God is useful before and after the earthly life of the individual: before, God grants us this precious viaticum, a conscience capable of distinguishing between good and evil, and a will enabling us to pursue the former and avoid the latter; after, at the Last Judgement, God distributes rewards and punishments. But, in the meantime, God withdraws and observes human struggles from afar, leaving us in sole command, subject to our own decisions.

Pelagius thought of himself as an orthodox Christian, but we might well ask if his doctrine can still be subsumed under the heading of religion rather than of a rule of conduct or an ethics. Since God has given his grace to all members of the human race, it is not really

necessary to be a Christian for salvation: there are
virtuous pagans who are saved, too. The first quality
required of humans is not submission – to dogma or to
the church – but self-control and strength of character;
not humility, but taking your destiny into your hands,
in other words autonomy. The god of Pelagius recalls
Prometheus, the Greek Titan who brought fire to men,
and therefore allowed them to control their own lives.
From this point of view, Pelagius – a somewhat severe
sage – is more reminiscent of the wise men of antiquity
than of Christians who obey their pastors, submit to the
authority of an institution (the church) and passively
await divine grace. Closer in this regard to the Stoics
than to any pious preachers, he relies more on purely
human means to move us forward on the path of salvation: education, social support, individual efforts.

Since human beings are not afflicted by any innate
failure, by original sin, they do not face any limits in
their efforts to improve themselves: the divine ideal is
not inaccessible. In support of this conclusion, Pelagius
cites a famous book of his time, the *Sentences* of
Rufinus. In it we read: 'God has granted men freedom
of will in order that by living purely and without sin
they may become like God.' There are, it is true, in both
the Old and the New Testament formulas that envisage
men becoming like God: 'Be ye therefore perfect, even
as your Father which is in heaven is perfect' (Matthew
5:48) or, 'Is it not written in your law, I said, Ye are
gods?' (John 10:34, referring to Psalm 82:6). But the
sense that Pelagius and Rufinus give this formula is
stronger, and does not simply imply we should imitate
the divine example: with regard to the management of
his own life, man has powers comparable to those of
God, and he will be the creator of his own being. If anything, it is the words of the serpent that come to mind
at this point, when it encouraged Eve to taste the fruits
of the tree of knowledge of good and evil: 'in the day ye

eat thereof, then your eyes shall be opened, and ye shall be as gods' (Genesis 3:5). But these were the very same words that led to original sin!

As the goal is so sublime, no effort, no sacrifice is too much; the reward will be eternal glory. Pelagius is a demanding master, and does not accept the usual excuses that his fellow citizens come up with for the lax lives they lead. Progress is within our reach, God has given us the power, we just need to add the will. Perfection is accessible to human beings, and so they must aspire to it. All must abide by certain rules of conduct, but those who want to attain the good face higher demands. Pelagius wrote a long letter to a girl, Demetria, who was destined by her family to marry but who had decided to dedicate her life to Christ while remaining a virgin. He encourages her unreservedly. The rich must immediately give their possessions to the poor. Those who fail to do so have no excuse and will receive the appropriate punishment. For breaking the command not to eat a certain food, Adam and Eve were doomed to become mortal, so how can we escape a harsh punishment for more serious sins? Anyway, we are unlikely to gain any favour on the grounds that the sin committed is not serious. Do people believe, exclaims Pelagius, that the fire that awaits the wicked in hell burns more or less fiercely for different categories of sinners? All will burn until the end of time for not having seized their chance to become as gods.

Pelagius has an optimistic view of human capabilities; for this very reason, his demands are very stringent. If an individual fails, he has no excuse, there is no point in blaming God, Providence, society or circumstances: he has only himself to blame, it is all his own fault. If his defeat is accompanied by a sense of shame or a nervous breakdown, this is no more than he deserves. On the other hand, if this individual does not merely work towards his own perfection, but decides that it is his responsibility to encourage his relatives or fellow

citizens to be perfect too, you can imagine the consequences: no sacrifice demanded – from *them*, this time
– will be too great. Since some people believe they are as
gods, who could blame them for forcing others, weaker
than they are, to follow the same path? Is it not worth
making the effort, when the reward is so great?

Augustine: the unconscious and original sin

Augustine, the bishop of Hippo, dedicated his life to
the church. Seeing that Pelagius did not give the church
any particular importance and recommended that the
rich should give their goods directly to the poor rather
than entrust them to God's representatives on earth,
Augustine could not fail to be suspicious of him. And
it is to a systematic refutation of Pelagianism that he
devoted the last years of his life.

First, Augustine addresses the interpretation of human
psychology found in the writings of Pelagius. For the
latter, human behaviour can be entirely subject to the
will. He thinks that man is completely transparent to
himself, perfectly accessible to his consciousness and
his will, without any distance between what he is and
what he wants. This is a serious mistake, Augustine
replies. The author of the *Confessions* has for years
scrutinized his own being and knows that this is not the
case: 'yet is there something of man, which neither the
spirit of man that is in him, itself knoweth' (X, 5); 'nor
do I myself comprehend all that I am. Therefore is the
mind too strait to contain itself' (X, 8). 'For that also is
a mournful darkness whereby my abilities within me are
hidden from me' (X, 32).[4] Not all our desires are conscious, we do not have access to our entire being: thus
our behaviour is not the effect of the will alone. We are
not in control of the forces that act within us. 'For of a
forward will, was a lust made; and a lust served, became

custom; and custom not resisted, became necessity'
(VIII, 5). The being that we are can choose what it wants
– but we do not choose our being, we are not a creation
of our will. The central example given by Augustine of
these unconscious motives is the attraction we feel for
a person, friend or lover: we do not love those we have
chosen, but we choose those we love.

As he is not the master in his own home, and does not
know the nature of the forces that drive him, the human
being cannot rely on his will, or demand that it lead
him to salvation. Freedom is not an illusion, but we are
never entirely free; at most we can move towards greater
freedom, and be freer today than yesterday. Man will
never attain divine freedom.

The attempt to control our unconscious impulses
fully, to overcome human powerlessness permanently,
leads to what Augustine called original sin. The concept was already present in Paul's epistles, but it was
Augustine who developed the doctrine in his fight
against Pelagius. Original sin is a lack or a weakness
found in any individual of the human race, inherited
at birth – it is thus a fundamental defect, independent
of his will and of his efforts to overcome it. Augustine
sometimes suggested that this defect is the presence
within us of ardent and irrepressible desires, or concu-
piscence: sexual libido, gluttony, lust. But original sin
itself, that of Adam and Eve, was not the result of such a
desire, but stemmed rather from the breaking of a single
command: not to taste the fruit of the tree of knowledge.
Having chosen to learn for themselves what constitutes
good and evil, and thus become capable of directing
their own existence, our first parents committed a sin:
they rejected obedience and opted for autonomy. Thus,
St Paul says that 'by one man's disobedience many
were made sinners' (Romans 5:19). Original sin is the
choice of pride at the expense of humility; it is the rejection of external authorities and the desire to be one's

own master. In asserting that men can save themselves, Pelagius reiterates and glorifies original sin. No wonder that Augustine opposed him.

For Augustine, the ways of salvation are completely different. No man can be freed by his own efforts. Salvation is possible, however, and man's helplessness does not condemn him to burn eternally in hell; the first step is to embrace the Christian religion. By dying on the cross, Jesus redeemed the human race; by joining the church through baptism, we take a first step towards salvation. The next step is to submit our conduct to the dictates of the church: it is obedience that saves us and the aspiration to greater autonomy that destroys us. Strength comes from faith, not from will or reason. Finally, it is not on human freedom that we need to rely if we are to be saved, but on the grace of God, a grace that man can neither summon nor predict. God's ways are inscrutable, and it is not enough to accumulate virtuous actions to obtain grace. As a Jansenist formula would summarize it centuries later, 'God owes us nothing': salvation is not a prize awarded to good students. Personal initiative is useless and even harmful: it is better to submit to the dogma, in other words the tradition. If we give up the attempt to be guided by ourselves, we will end up loving the good that authority points to, and exercising our freedom to move in the direction indicated by the commands we have been given.

Man is helpless and doomed to remain so: Augustine's vision is much less optimistic than that of Pelagius. But when it comes to the demands made of mankind, Augustine is substantially more accommodating than his rival. It is true that, as a priest and bishop, he was required to rub shoulders with the common people, while Pelagius had surrounded himself with chosen disciples already engaged on a personal quest. Augustine believed that everyone starts off with a heavy handicap, being hampered by original sin, but often by adverse circumstances as well – a hostile environment, their own ignorance. Their strength is limited, their knowledge still incomplete: one should not be too harsh on their failures. The Christian church welcomes everyone, and is not reserved only for elite personalities. Not all people are able to stand on their own two feet, but all are able to obey. For Pelagius, the ideal man is an adult, someone who has attained full independence. For Augustine, men are children who do not know themselves or conceal themselves because they are ashamed of their dependency and weakness: they are babies in the arms of God. Perfection is inaccessible to them, and so their sins will be forgiven.

The outcome of the debate

In the public debates of the time, Augustine's arguments outweighed those of Pelagius. In 418, the ideas of the latter were declared heretical, his disciples were condemned, excommunicated and expelled; we lose track of Pelagius himself, and he probably died soon after. The controversy was rekindled a few years later, when a disciple of Pelagius, Julian of Eclanum, in turn attacked Augustine: but the bishop of Hippo defended himself stoutly. In 431, following Augustine's death, a new council strongly condemned Pelagianism – once and for all, it was hoped at the time. Heteronomy, or submission to a law imposed from elsewhere, outweighed autonomy, the law that one gives oneself.

One may wonder, however, if the canker was not still in the bud. To return to the starting point of Pelagian thinking, God created man in his own image. Now the God of monotheism has a feature that distinguishes him radically from the gods of pagan religions; he does not find an existing universe into which he introduces order, he is the creator of the universe itself; the world is the result of a free act of his will. In Pelagius, man resembles God much more than in Augustine. Moreover, God commands man to act as master and possessor of nature, to submit the rest of the universe to his will: 'Be fruitful, and multiply, and replenish the earth, and subdue it: and have dominion over the fish of the sea, and over the fowl of the air, and over every living thing that moveth upon the earth' (Genesis 1:30). (Not a very ecological commandment!) And God acts alone, without interaction with others (since there are no others of his kind); so man is also destined to act alone, regardless of the human environment or society that shapes him.

Today we tend to think that it is actually man who has created God in his own image – the God of the Gospels even more than that of Genesis, since, even before creating the universe, God possesses the Word, and so is similar to man, who, by the power given him by language, can shape the world in his own way: 'In the beginning was the Word, and the Word was with God, and the Word was God' (John 1:1). But this means that, at the time he came up with these stories, man had an image of himself which resembled the one he would attribute to God: the image of a being capable of creating, by an effort of his will, the world around him. When the Pelagians say that men can become like God, they are just finding a vivid expression of their conception of man, master of his fate and the rest of the universe. Not only does man create God in his image, he also wants to form man in the image of a free creator. The autonomy ascribed to God is a first form of the autonomy that man claims for himself. The words in Genesis help us finally understand, in a thoroughly Pelagian spirit, that man creates himself and that his will knows no limits. This is why, despite the victory of the Augustinians, their debate with the Pelagians can never end: religion asks men *both* to submit to God (and to his servants on earth, in other words the church) *and* to try to be like God, acting as free, self-determined subjects who shape their own destiny.

This is not the place to enter into the details of this debate, one of the most important in Christian history. The official dogma of the church is still the one bequeathed by Augustine, but throughout the history of Christianity, it has been necessary to combat the rebels, those who ascribe too active a role to man. They are suspected of being contaminated by the Pelagian or at least 'semi-Pelagian' heresy. 'Fundamentalist' Christians take a stand against this deviation. For Luther, it is inconceivable that man can ensure his salvation by his own efforts. The Jansenist controversy was fought out on the same ground: when Pascal describes man after the Fall, you can hear in his words the reproaches addressed to the Pelagians. Pascal imagines God saying that man 'wanted to make himself his own centre, independent of my help. He withdrew from my domination and, as he made himself equal to me in his desire to find his happiness in himself, I abandoned him to himself.'[5] Calvin, as shown by Louis Dumont, forged a remarkable synthesis of the two views. By bringing the individual with his values into the social world, by interpreting his submission to divine grace as an act of will, man shapes himself in the image of God. In this way, Calvin contributes to modern Prometheanism.[6]

In parallel with this, from the Renaissance onwards, non-religious authors engaged in a defence of human abilities, which is why they are known as humanists. Among the opponents of Augustinian pessimism about human nature we find, for example, Pico della Mirandola, whose thinking is similar to that of Pelagius, even if he does not mention him: Pico's God speaks to man in terms very different from those transcribed by Pascal: 'you may, as the free and proud shaper of your own being, fashion yourself in the form you may prefer'. A few years later, in the early sixteenth century,

Erasmus, who knew Pelagius but needed to differentiate himself from him, nonetheless affirmed that 'God created free will' and added: 'But what does man achieve in addition, if our will is to God as a vase to a potter?' Montaigne, at the end of the century, cherished 'our own choice and voluntary freedom' and the soul that can 'choose and discern of itself'.[7] In the following century, Descartes praised free will: 'For we can be rightly praised or blamed only for actions that depend on this free will; it makes us *like God* in a way, by making us masters of ourselves.'[8] At the same time, he thought that the world is completely knowable, and thus paved the way for modern science and technology. This faith in man as being able to direct his destiny spread among Descartes' followers: in the second half of the eighteenth century, a German historian and philologist, Johann Salomo Semler, would for the first time publicly take sides with Pelagius against Augustine.

Enlightenment thought was in its turn closer to Pelagius, but it should be noted immediately that this thought did not form a homogeneous unity. What we mean by 'Enlightenment' was not a rational and coherent doctrine, where the consequences followed from rigorous, universally accepted principles; rather, it was a broad discussion which combined contradictory or complementary proposals, either inherited from the past or newly formulated. It was a debate that took advantage of the widespread and accelerated flow of ideas between individuals and between countries. Voltaire attacked Rousseau who criticized Diderot – yet all three were part of the Enlightenment. When we are discussing Enlightenment thought, we need to be more specific.

The greatest representatives of humanist thought in France held, on the issue of human nature and the power of the will, a position that cannot be reduced to either of the two doctrines from antiquity (though they were aware of these doctrines). It is true that, like

Pelagius, they do not recommend total submission to public authorities, or to the values derived from tradition or the supposed intentions of Providence: rather, they believe that the individual can improve himself, just as he can improve the society in which he lives. Instead of relying solely on his predestination, he must contribute to his own salvation. These thinkers are on the side of autonomy. It is the nature of men, Montesquieu wrote at the beginning of *The Spirit of Laws*, that they must be able to act as 'free agents', adding: 'every man who is supposed [to be] a free agent ought to be his own governor'.[9] Of course, Rousseau opens his *Social Contract* with the gloomy observation that he sees man everywhere in chains even though he was born free: this characteristic was part of the very definition of man: 'To renounce your liberty is to renounce your status as a man.' As opposed to Christian traditionalists, he does not believe that, in order to go to heaven, it is enough to be baptized, to comply with the rituals of the church and to wait for grace: 'And I think, on the contrary, that what is essential in Religion consists in practice; and that not only must one be a good man, merciful, humane, and charitable, but that anyone who is truly like that has enough belief for being saved.'[10] Human works rather than divine grace lead to salvation.

At the same time, in their anthropological views, these authors are closer to Augustine than to Pelagius. They believe that the human being is hampered by internal obstacles that he has the greatest difficulty in overcoming; they do not believe in linear progress, or the possibility for men to attain perfection: evil cannot be eradicated once and for all.

Montesquieu shows that men tend to be blind about themselves, and are prey to impulses they cannot manage. 'But constant experience shows us that every man invested with power is apt to abuse it.'[11] This omnipresent temptation weighs no less than original sin, and it is related to it: it shows that there is always the danger of unlimited confidence in one's own abilities. Montesquieu has another reason to reserve a special place for moderation in his conception of the human world. He believes in universal values and therefore the possibility of trans-cultural judgements, since his typology of political regimes does not depend on the circumstances of their lives; so he can condemn despotism wherever it is found and consider it to be the epitome of a 'monstrous government'. He knows, however, that the customs of different nations are infinitely variable and cannot be evaluated using a single criterion. Accordingly, he asks us to accept the plurality of societies and temper our reforming zeal: judgements may well be universal, but action must be adapted to each particular case. The task of politics is to reconcile the conflicting interests of different sectors of society, by offering all of them reasonable compromises; its aims are relative, not absolute.

According to Rousseau, the same function of acting as a brake on any overweening ambition is provided by the fact that men necessarily live among others. Contrary to what a widespread image of his doctrine would suggest, Rousseau does not see the human being in isolation: existential solitude, that is to say indifference to the way others see us, was the lot of our animal ancestors, those who came before hominization. The 'vocation of mankind', as Rousseau called it, is to live in society, and an isolated individual is bound to be 'a ferocious animal'. Alas, this state, through which men have become fully human, does not fail to 'inspire all men with a wicked inclination to injure each other'. We can never hope to be rid of this characteristic, and it is not necessary: we would lose our humanity. Rousseau sees in this duality the fundamental character of the human condition, which he describes in this formula: 'Good and evil flow from the same source', namely sociability, the fact that we inevitably depend on others.[12] He also knows that improvements in one area are paid for by regressions in another: the efforts of the will are not automatically rewarded. 'Subsequent progress was in appearance one step towards the perfecting of the individual, but in reality it hastened the decay of the species.'

In a word, neither Montesquieu nor Rousseau thought that man could be fully known by his own reason and controlled by his will. It follows that any dream of perfection, like that of Pelagius, is ruled out of court by these thinkers. Montesquieu condemns despotism, but the principle he sets up against it is moderation, a balance of powers, not the reign of virtue. Rousseau comes to a similar conclusion, albeit by a completely different path – through resignation, not through choice. We should here remember that the *Social Contract* does not describe a utopia to be brought into existence, but the principles of political right that enable us to analyse and evaluate existing states. At the same time, both authors continued to claim that man had and should have the right to decide freely on his own behaviour. So there is absolutely no question of denying this impulse, only one of showing that it is always limited, and that this limit must in turn be respected. In practice, these Enlightenment thinkers accepted the imperfection of the world and the people in it, though they did not give up the attempt to improve them; however, rather than waiting for divine grace, they preferred to appeal to human beings to take responsibility for this themselves. So they opted for a middle way, which rejected both conservative fatalism and the dream of total mastery. Humanism properly speaking has this twofold characteristic: it believes *both* in the power of the will *and* in moderation. The better is possible, but perfection lies beyond our reach.

3

Political Messianism

Turin, 17 September 1863. During dinner, Fyodor Mikhailovich, looking at a girl who was having lessons, told me: 'Well, imagine a girl like this, with an old man, and there's a Napoleon who comes along and says "Kill everyone in the whole city." In this world, things have always happened that way.'

Apollinaria Suslova, *Diary*

The revolutionary moment

At the end of the eighteenth century, the Pelagian legacy, now back in favour, underwent a twofold change in French society. First, there was less concern about the fate of individuals, and more focus on societies; less morals, and more politics. This is also true of both Rousseau and Montesquieu. The former describes the need for individual autonomy, and even dreams of individual autarky, but at the same time, he emphasizes the need for the sovereignty of the people, sole master of their destiny. The second is interested in political systems and legislation; original sin and individual salvation are not his concerns. Secondly, there is a gradual shift from learned debates between theologians and philosophers to political actions and speeches addressed to the powerful of this world, or else to the crowd. The demand for autonomy emerges from the academies and salons and is debated out on the streets; the struggle is led, not by scholars, but by men engaged in the public arena. In this way, the issues first mooted in private and personal publications led to the French Revolution.

In the years leading up to the outbreak of the Revolution, the moderate attitude, as it could be seen in the thought of Montesquieu (and even Rousseau), was subjected to strong criticism from other representatives of the Enlightenment, thus introducing a real split in this line of thought. The iconic figure here is Condorcet, who wrote a commentary on the work of Montesquieu. On the crucial issue of the appropriate legislation for each country, he condemned the pluralism of his predecessor and what he saw as his conservatism. If, through science and reason, it has been established what the right laws must be, why not give these laws to all people? More generally, we find in Condorcet an optimism of the will: in a thoroughly Pelagian spirit he thinks that, if we apply ourselves to the task, we will be able to eradicate evil from the face of the earth; the march of progress will continue indefinitely, and all men will one day lead lives of fulfilment. Faith in continuous and unlimited progress, a faith of which Condorcet is one of the main promoters, applies to mankind as a whole the individual's capacity for development, affirmed by Pelagius. Here, within the Enlightenment, we move from what might seem like a 'wait and see' attitude (that of Montesquieu) to a spirited activism.

The shifts in the themes and place of the debate blended with the voluntarism of Condorcet, and together they provided an appropriate framework for the ardent longings that were now widespread. The new thinking found favour with the protagonists of the Revolution. Moreover, Condorcet would be one of them: no longer satisfied with being secretary of the French Academy, he decided to move from scientific and philosophical reflection to political action, becoming, in 1791, an active member of the Legislative Assembly.

In moving from the individual to the communal field and freeing itself from its earlier religious framework, the Pelagian project had radicalized itself. The idea spread that the human will, provided it becomes the common will, can enable the good to rule and bring salvation to all; and this happy event will not happen in heaven after death, but here and now. Thus, voluntarism joined forces with certain religious heresies of the past, millenarian or messianic, that promised an imminent radical transformation of the world – except that, now, the nature of these objectives was strictly secular. If there is a messiah, he is a collective character, the people – an abstraction that allows some individuals to present themselves as his incarnation. The renunciation of any sacred sphere of supernatural origin facilitates the rise of a new hope. Men imagine that the world can be transformed in accordance with their desires, and their willingness to act is multiplied: now, everything is allowed and everything is possible. Like the Pelagians, revolutionaries believe that no obstacle should be placed in the way of the infinite progression of mankind; original sin is a superstition that must be rejected. Societies have a past, admittedly, but they have no obligation to submit to tradition. This attitude is exemplified in certain words of Jean-Paul Rabaut Saint-Étienne, a member of the Constituent Assembly: 'We draw on history; but history is not our law [code].'[1] This does not mean that our behaviour must lie outside any regulations, but it must be based on the principles of reason and justice alone.

The goal is to produce a new society and a new man. Existing human beings are viewed as a shapeless mass that an effort of the will can lead to perfection. The task of making all men both virtuous and happy suddenly seems within reach. In the first place, we must provide ourselves with good laws. Revolutionary France consumed constitutions at a breakneck pace. Condorcet himself put one such constitution forward; in the public debate on it, Saint-Just, a prominent political figure, proposed his own project, in which he laid out a major role for the Assembly which he was addressing. His words are worth recalling: 'The Legislator commands the future; there is no point in his being weak; it is for him to will the good and to perpetuate it; it is for him to make men what he wants them to be.'[2] The malleable human material is placed in the hands of the legislator, that is to say of the members of the Assembly, or rather those who control them. Once the good has been attained, it will of course need to be 'perpetuated': in other words, the use of violence cannot stop, the Revolution will be followed by the Terror. This does not result by happenstance, but from the very structure of the project. As the highest good is at stake, all paths taken to reach it are good ('there is no point in his being weak') and we are entitled to destroy those who oppose it, as they have ipso facto become an incarnation of evil: obstacles can only come from a bad will. The next step will be the transformation of this means into an end: Terror and the state institutions it requires will absorb all the forces of power, and the guillotine will never rest (Rabaut Saint-Étienne will be one of its victims, Saint-Just another).

We see that, while claiming to draw on the ideal of equality and freedom, what I call here (to remind us of its religious origins) political messianism – a messianism without a messiah – had its own final goal (establishing the equivalent of heaven on earth), as well as specific ways to achieve it (Revolution and Terror). In its quest for a temporal salvation, this doctrine holds no place for God, but preserves other features of the ancient religion, such as blind faith in the new dogmas, fervent belief in the actions that serve it and the proselytizing of the faithful, and the transformation of its fallen supporters into martyr figures to be worshipped as saints. Attempts to impose a cult of the Supreme Being and create a festival celebrating this Being were part of the same trend. Condorcet, who had fought the old religion, was alarmed at the result, even though it was the product of a process he had helped to initiate – what he called 'a kind of political religion'.[3] The fusion of temporal power and spiritual power dreamt by the Revolution led, a few years later, to the emergence of corresponding projects of counter-revolutionary theocracy (quite different from the French state before 1789). The future would show that Condorcet's anxieties were not misplaced.

The first wave: revolutionary and colonial wars

In European history, political (or secular) messianism went through several distinct phases.

The first of these began in the aftermath of 1789. The peak period of the French Revolution was short, and neither society nor individuals had time to be transformed in depth. But the revolutionary project was transferred to its armies, who were given the task of carrying it beyond France's borders: the revolution was a war conducted at home, while war was a continuation of the revolution in other countries. It might even be easier to impose the good on other people than on those at home; the war situation meant you did not need to be hampered by internal resistance. 'The French people is voting for the freedom of the world', said Saint-Just. In 1792, the Convention had already decided to grant 'fraternity and aid to all peoples who wish to recover their liberty';[4] in practice, this meant that the occupation of their country by French soldiers was legitimate. The proponents of revolutionary wars, especially the group of Girondins, including Condorcet, demanded that fraternity be exported everywhere, by force of arms if necessary; only in this way could one really achieve the higher goal of perpetual peace. Condorcet was convinced that the French soldiers, taking revolutionary principles with them, would be feted by foreign peoples. Brissot, another member of the group, said: 'The moment has come for a new crusade, and it has a far nobler, and holier object. It is a crusade for universal liberty.'[5] None of these supporters of freedom for all wondered whether deciding the future of other peoples in this way might not violate the principle of universal equality which they defended elsewhere.

The goal was placed so high that all means should be employed: the elimination of enemies became a secondary issue. 'The hirelings of despotism will be vanquished by the exterminating angel of liberty', predicted Danton, referring to foreign populations. The destruction of the enemy was no longer an inconvenience, but rather a moral duty. Violence was not disguised, it was openly demanded. Carnot, a revolutionary general, started out from this premise: 'War is a violent state of affairs. It must be waged to the utmost.' Revolutionary violence was met by counter-revolutionary atrocities in an endless spiral. It was in this spirit that repression in the Vendée, in early 1794, would be carried out. The revolution was in danger, the supreme good might not be attained: we should not pity the fates of our enemies. The rules of good behaviour were immediately forgotten. 'It is horrifying,' wrote a French captain who took part in punitive expeditions, 'but the wellbeing of the Republic requires it imperiously' (i.e. the killing of civilians). Another officer said: 'It is out of a principle of humanity that I am purging the land of liberty of these monsters.'[6]

After his accession to power, Napoleon endorsed the same ideology; thus France experienced, and imposed on the rest of Europe, twenty-three years of continuous wars (1792–1815), responsible for millions of victims. On the domestic level, Napoleon preserved some of the Revolution's gains, and eliminated others; but in the international arena, he chose to present himself systematically as the heir of the Enlightenment and the Revolution, and relied on the force of attraction of their values. As Germaine de Staël said, Napoleon was a Robespierre on horseback. The newspaper that he published during his campaign in Italy states: 'The conquests of a free nation improve the lot of the vanquished, decrease the power of kings, and increase enlightenment.' Once the regiments of Napoleon's army had occupied Spain, Marshal Murat wrote to his emperor: 'Your Majesty is awaited here like the Messiah.'[7]

The reality was quite different: after a brief period in which the local population was relieved to see its former oppressors driven out of power, disillusionment quickly followed; the new tyranny was even more bitter as it was imposed by foreigners. The violence inflicted by resistance fighters would equal the violence they suffered. Masséna, another of Napoleon's marshals, admitted that, during the crackdown in Italy, 'excessive acts that were impossible to avoid' had been committed 'in order to achieve victory'. It must be said that the Italian insurgents, for their part, did not hesitate to roast alive those whom they suspected of pro-French sympathies. The same happened in Spain, where the word guerrilla was now forged to describe the actions of the resistance fighters. The occupiers were pursued with a hatred every bit as intense as their own desire to impose the good: 'What sort of thing is a Frenchman? A monstrous, undefinable half-created creature. Everyone has the right to kill this ferocious animal.'[8]

The French revolutionaries felt politically superior to their contemporaries in other European countries; compared to more distant countries in Africa, Asia and America, they had the impression of a more radical superiority because they placed themselves at the summit of civilization. All peoples, Condorcet wrote, must 'one day approach the state of civilization reached by the most enlightened peoples, those who are freest and least hampered by prejudice, such as the French and the Anglo-Americans'. This should lead to the gradual disappearance of 'the immense distance that separates these people from the bondage of the Indians, the barbarity of the African tribes, and the ignorance of savages'. It was in the name of the ideal of equality that Condorcet wished to transform the lives of these distant populations: his duty as a civilized man was to free them from barbarism. But they themselves might not be aware of the good that awaited them, and might resist, in which case they should be forced, because, as Condorcet also said, the European population needed to 'civilize [them] or cause [them] to disappear'.[9]

The leaders of the most 'enlightened' countries would implement the dreams of Condorcet. England began to make inroads into the Indian peninsula in the last years of the century; for his part, Napoleon decided in 1798 to conquer Egypt. He harangued his troops at the moment of the attack: 'Soldiers, you are about to undertake a conquest whose effects on civilization and commerce are incalculable.' After the victory, he busied himself with modernizing the judicial system, communications and the economy, but as soon as the native population tried to regain its independence, he brutally repressed it. In Haiti, the news of the Revolution and the first decisions of the National Assembly encouraged the slaves to revolt; but in 1801, a French expeditionary force, led by the brother-in-law of Napoleon, Leclerc, landed on the island. He managed to arrest the rebel leader Toussaint Louverture, but could not stem the resistance of the former slaves, who wanted to rule themselves. Leclerc responded with drastic measures, writing to Napoleon:

'We must destroy all negroes of the mountains, men and women, keeping only children younger than twelve [. . .]. Without this, the colony will never be peaceful.'[10]

Napoleon did not build a colonial empire; in France, this would be the task of later generations. The conquest of Algeria, which started in 1830, ended in 1857; the final conquest of India was achieved by 1858, and the partition of Africa and the rest of Asia would be a fait accompli by the end of the century. The reference to revolutionary principles was no longer popular, but the idea of bringing civilization to the barbarians, and thus spreading enlightenment everywhere, was still important, and it served to legitimize both French and English conquests. Jules Ferry, president of the Council of Ministers in France, justified the expeditions he sent out in these terms: 'The superior races have a right vis-à-vis the inferior races [. . .] because they are duty bound. They have a duty to civilize the inferior races.'[11] It does not matter whether he himself believed or not in this argument, the bottom line was that it should be effective: young soldiers and, later, settlers would leave for the colonies with the certainty they were serving a noble mission.

The main features of political messianism thus fell into place: a noble programme; asymmetrical roles, with the active subject on one side and the passive beneficiary on the other (who was not asked for his opinion); and the military means made available to carry out the project.

The second wave: the Communist project

The overall shift of the messianic project – from the inside to the outside, from the transformation of one's own society to the war of liberation of others – did not prevent many followers of the Revolution regretting the way it was brought to a halt and dreaming of giving it a new start. This movement began in the aftermath of 9 Thermidor with the 'conspiracy of equals' led by Babeuf. 'The French Revolution', we read in the manifesto of the 'Equals', 'is only the forerunner of another revolution, much larger, much more solemn: it will be the last.'[12] In these formulas, we can see the emergence of the millenarian spirit – the time of the final battle is approaching – now translated into Communist terms. The conspiracy failed, but many other visionaries tried to imagine a continuation and radicalization of the failed revolution. Saint-Simon (a disciple of Condorcet) and Fourier, Proudhon and Louis Blanc, Herzen and Bakunin offered different variants of socialism. The version that would experience the most lasting success was the one developed, from the 1840s onwards, by two Germans living abroad, Karl Marx and Friedrich Engels, the founders of true Communism. A brochure published in London in 1848 was to have a lasting success: their *Manifesto of the Communist Party*.

This booklet describes in eloquent terms the conditions of life of the exploited classes, who have now become the equivalent of a pure commodity, and formulates the dream of a perfect society common to all men. Its analysis of past societies is based on the assumption that struggle is the only form of social interaction in the history of humanity: the main question is who will seize power and use it to exploit the other. There is nothing shared by all the members of a society, as everything belongs to one or other of the competing sides. There is no universal category: neither morality, nor justice, nor ideas, nor civilization. No religion, no tradition (including the family and private property) escapes its class origins.

This new phase of messianism took place at a time of general admiration for the achievements of science, illustrated by the contemporary industrial revolution. This gave birth to a doctrine, scientism, which should not be confused with science, and is even opposed to its whole spirit. This doctrine claims that the world can be fully known, and that it can thus be transformed in accordance with an ideal. This ideal, instead of being freely chosen, is a consequence of scientific knowledge as such. This worldview would be extended from inert matter, the subject of physics, to human history and the knowledge of society. Condorcet, in his *Sketch for a Historical Tableau of the Progress of the Human Mind*, thinks he can observe a direction in the course of history: it leads to the perfecting of the human species; so what happens is in reality an incarnation of what must be. That repressive governments and priests are seeing their power weaken is proof of the inexorable advance of history: its march necessarily brings us towards the good. This is also implied by an expression such as 'the court of history', suggesting that history would lay the foundations of a kind of right – as if the victory of the strongest were also the victory of the most just. A formula of Hegel's, borrowed from a poem by Schiller, sums up this view: '*Die Weltgeschichte ist das Weltgericht*' ('World history is the tribunal of the world'),[13] and it was adopted by the followers of Hegel, including the young Marx. Yet the word 'tribunal' in this expression has nothing more to do with justice than the word 'right' in 'might is right', or 'law' in the 'law of the jungle'.

Like all messianic movements, Communism defends the idea that history has a predetermined and unchangeable direction; Communism saw this as legitimizing its actions. Here we recognize the role that in Christianity was reserved for Providence, but now, in order to determine the direction in which we are travelling, it is not enough to read the scriptures, we must establish the laws of history in a scientific manner. For this reason, the Communists deny that their analysis and project are based on assumptions that could be submitted to examination, rather than on solid facts: as the *Communist Manifesto* puts it: 'The theoretical conclusions of the Communists are in no way based on ideas or principles that have been invented, or discovered, by this or that would-be universal reformer. They merely express, in general terms, actual relations springing from an existing class struggle.'[14] A phrase of Lenin, which was engraved on the monument to Marx in the centre of Moscow, puts it even better: 'Marxism is all-powerful because it is true.' It was because of this assumption that Marx and Engels would also be intolerant of any divergent opinion: it would be attacked not only as politically inappropriate, but as false and therefore not worthy of consideration.

The goal aimed at by Marxist 'science' is the disappearance of any differences between human groups, as each difference is perceived as a source of conflict, and ultimately a death struggle. This is why we need to abolish private property and place all instruments of production in the hands of the state. Those who resist will be removed, including the bourgeoisie, whose interests go in the opposite direction. 'The existence of the bourgeoisie is no longer compatible with society.' So we must engage in the 'abolition' of the bourgeois property-owner: 'This person must indeed be swept out of the way and made impossible.' The precise means of suppression are not detailed, but the *Manifesto* admits that 'despotic inroads' will be required, as the desired ends can be achieved 'only through the forcible overthrow of all existing social conditions'.[15] The physical elimination of the bourgeoisie as a class is already on the agenda. Either way, the transformation of society as envisaged by the *Manifesto* is so radical – the abolition of private property and the disappearance of classes – that it is inconceivable it might be achieved without bloodshed.

At first sight, therefore, we are here a world away from Pelagian, revolutionary voluntarism, since human action is entirely subject to laws over which men have no control. However, Marxism is not only a deterministic theory, it is also an intransigent voluntarism. The combination of these two seemingly contradictory characteristics is explained by the famous Marxist dogma that 'existence determines consciousness'. Consciousness, and therefore the will of individuals, is bound to act in the direction foreseen by the laws of history, because consciousness is their product. The will necessarily supports being.

For several decades, the followers of Marxist doctrine led a marginal and sometimes underground existence, or organized socialist groups and parties that were obliged to remain in opposition. It was during this period, however, that Lenin, in Russia, made his own decisive contribution: in his view, a lucid elite could identify the desirable course of history (in earlier times they would have called this 'the ways of Providence'), and by concerted action could bring about the events that would comply with it. Without saying so, Lenin reversed the Marxist adage. It was now the turn of consciousness to determine existence; voluntarism outweighed determinism.[16] Thus, the fact that, according to the Marxist laws of history, the revolution must occur first in an industrialized country could now be ignored. Russia was a backward and peasant country, but it had the most combative party, so it was here that the world revolution must begin. The fight would now no longer be led by the workers themselves, but by the party, composed of professional revolutionaries from the bourgeoisie and the intelligentsia, devoted body and soul to the cause. The dictatorship of the proletariat would be necessary to transform society according to a pre-established programme. This overturning of the doctrine would mean the real state of the country could be overlooked in favour of successive fictions, depending on the needs of the party at every stage of history.

In 1917, in the context of World War I, a new stage began: for the first time, thanks to the Bolshevik coup d'état, the spiritual power claimed by the original faithful was backed up by the temporal power proper to a large state, Russia. This gave rise to the period of expansion of this form of messianism, this attempt to introduce utopia into reality, which created a unique social formation, the totalitarian state. The rest is history: the rise in Europe of another form of totalitarianism, Nazism, produced in part by the same structural causes as Communism, but also posing as a shield or weapon against it. Here, scientism no longer appealed to the laws of history, but to those of biology, which the Nazis discovered in a version of Social Darwinism adapted to their needs. On the basis of its supposed achievements, they could quietly contemplate the disappearance of the 'inferior races'. There followed the complicity between the two forms of totalitarianism and then the war to the death between them, won by the alliance between the Soviet Union and the Western democracies.

Communism supplants and sometimes combats the messianism that had preceded it, consisting of imperialist wars in the name of liberty, equality and fraternity, and colonial conquests in the name of European civilization. Yet both belong to the same 'genus', and this kinship helps us identify the specificity of Communist utopianism. First, the messianism that emerged from the French Revolution seeks, essentially, to bring salvation to *others*: to other European nations, in the case of Napoleon, and to the inhabitants of other continents during the colonial wars. Communist utopianism, on the other hand, is directed initially at the home affairs of each country: the war that must lead to its triumph is a civil war between classes; on the international level, it recommended an expansion and generalization of these civil wars rather than the subjugation of one country by another (on this point, Soviet practice betrayed its theory). Secondly, revolutionary messianism proposes to constrain and educate the peoples who are reluctant to embrace its creed, but not to destroy them – it is a gradual and progressive project. The victims of the revolution or war which lead to this goal can be very numerous, but killing them is 'collateral damage', not a goal in itself. Communist utopianism is different: it requires the disappearance of its opponents, and it is easier to imagine this in the context of a civil war than in a war between countries. In other words, organs of terror such as the Cheka and the extermination of entire segments of the population are made possible, even necessary, by the Communist project itself.

Imagining an ideal in whose name we try to transform reality, dreaming up a transcendence that allows us to criticize the existing world in order to improve it, is probably a feature common to all mankind; it is not enough in itself to produce messianism. What characterizes the latter more specifically is the form assumed by the drive towards perfection: all the aspects of the life of a people are involved. Not content with changing institutions, it aspires to transforming human beings themselves; and with this aim, it does not hesitate to resort to arms. What distinguishes the totalitarian project, finally, is both the content of the ideal proposed and the strategy chosen to impose it: the total control of society, and the elimination of whole categories of the population.

This last feature is what makes totalitarian messianism so radically different both from its predecessor and from its successors, even though they were all formed in the same womb: the Pelagian precepts that were revived in the Enlightenment and transformed into a programme for collective action. Whatever the particular version of totalitarianism, this systematic destruction would always be at work, while it was absent elsewhere:

this is true of the extermination of the kulaks as a class in the Soviet Union, of Jews in Nazi Germany, of the bourgeoisie in Mao's China, and of urban dwellers in the Communist regime of Pol Pot. Together with this came the abuse and suffering inflicted on the rest of the population, also incommensurable with those previously experienced. It is important to keep in mind both the similarities and the obvious differences.

At the same time, and even more strikingly, the Communist project opposed the dominant spirit of the society of its time. This society included many ingredients from the past, some of them, indeed, remnants of the old regime; but its overall orientation, fostered by the industrial revolution and the expansion of trade, was liberal. This meant, among other things, that the place of religion shrank every day and so society tended to lose any relation to an absolute. Liberalism encouraged personal development, but offered no new common ideal – as if the rapid development of technology and the accumulation of wealth were sufficient to make up for the disappearance of religion. Communist messianism would step into the vacuum, and would in turn embody the absolute – with the added advantage that it announced its imminent triumph.

For a brief period following the end of World War II, Communist messianism continued to expand. Basking in its victory over Nazi Germany, the Soviet Union extended its empire to Eastern Europe, increased its popularity in Western Europe, and encouraged the revolutions carried out in the name of the same ideal in Asia (China, Korea, Vietnam), declaring itself to be the ally of all anti-colonial movements. From the death of Stalin in 1953, a decline set in. Inside the country, the utopian spirit of the early days and the fanaticism that accompanied it were displaced by the desire for power for power's sake, the reign of careerist cynicism, by bureaucracy and corruption. Outside the Soviet Union, for a few years, the United States and other Western powers had prevented the empire from expanding by engaging in a 'cold war'. In Asia, the Communist countries chose to emancipate themselves from Soviet control; conflicts thus arose within the same camp. In Eastern Europe, any messianic hopes crumbled before the reality of Communist regimes, and only surveillance, accompanied by systematic repression, ensured their survival.

I lived under this regime for twenty years. What is most deeply engraved in my memory is not the countless problems of daily life, or even the constant surveillance and the lack of freedom. What I remember, most of all, is an acute awareness of this paradox: all this evil was done in the name of good, was justified by a goal presented as sublime.

The third wave: imposing democracy by bombs

Since the fall of the Communist empire in Europe in the years 1989–91, there has been a third form of political messianism – which is the first to correspond to modern democracies. It is opposed in many respects to the totalitarian projects that preceded it, but has some similarities with the first wave of revolutionary and colonial wars. This policy consists in imposing democracy and human rights by force – though this is a move which generates an internal threat to the democratic countries themselves.

The Western states which embody this project present it as a fulfilment of democracy, and not as a breach of its principles, as the Communist project avowedly was. However, we can observe a certain continuity between the messianism of the second and third waves, again brought out by the similarity between the protagonists in both cases. Sometimes this education can take a whole generation. Thus, many American 'neocons'

(a confusing term because they are not actually conservative), the ideologues of military intervention on
behalf of human rights, are drawn from the formerly
pro-Communist intelligentsia that has in the meanwhile
converted to anti-Stalinism (first of a Trotskyist, then
of a democratic stamp). In France, the same individuals will sometimes have carried out this manoeuvre in
three steps: having been followers of the Communist
religion before or shortly after 1968, often in one of
its extreme left-wing variants, they became radically
anti-Communist and anti-totalitarian a few years later
as a result of the dissemination of new information on
the reality of the gulag (whereupon they took the name
nouveaux philosophes), then appearing, in recent years,
as the proponents of 'democratic' or 'humanitarian'
war in Iraq, Afghanistan and Libya. In the countries of
Eastern Europe, we find the same continuity (not in all
cases, of course). The typical course is that of the young
'idealistic' Communist of the early stages (phase I) who,
disappointed by the reality disguised by the slogans,
turns into a courageous dissident (phase II), becoming, after the fall of the regime, an active zealot for the
'humanitarian bombs' dropped on Belgrade during
the war in Kosovo, or the defence of the West during the
wars in Iraq and Afghanistan (phase III).

The first manifestation of this new form of messianism
was NATO's intervention in the conflict in Yugoslavia
in 1999, in which the central government in Belgrade
was opposed to the Albanian-speaking province of
Kosovo. It is no coincidence that the confrontation took
place after the end of the Cold War: the Soviet Union
was no longer there to prevent it. The Western countries
which initiated it did not seek to obtain authorization
from international bodies such as the UN, which in any
case does not have its own armed wing. This intervention was based on a doctrine formulated at the same
time, after the Rwandan genocide of 1994, in many

Western countries, particularly in France: the 'right to intervene'. Subscribing to this doctrine amounts to saying that if there are human rights violations in a country, the other countries in the world have the right to enter that country by force to protect the victims and prevent the abusers from acting.

In Yugoslavia, the application of these principles revealed several difficulties inherent in the doctrine. Some concern uncertainties in the relevant information: each of the two opposing forces has an interest in inflating the number of victims and concealing its own acts of aggression (data manipulation is a shared temptation). In this respect, the Albanian-speaking minority, which managed to secure the support of American diplomacy and of NATO, was more effective than the Serb majority. A second difficulty comes from the necessarily selective application of the principle: human rights violations are unfortunately very numerous, and it is impossible to intervene everywhere, so we choose to side with our political friends and pit our strength against those who follow a policy that goes against our interests – thus undermining the impartiality of choice. A third difficulty stems from the actual shape taken by interference, namely war with its inevitable consequences: bombardments, the destruction of the country and its people, untold suffering. To save ten innocents do we have the right to kill a hundred others?

I will not go into the details of this episode in recent history.[17] I will simply recall that NATO's military intervention in Yugoslavia ended, unsurprisingly, in the military victory of the Alliance; Kosovo gained political independence without quite becoming a state under the rule of law, as it is still plagued by criminal gangs; ethnic discrimination, of which Albanian-speakers were victims at the hands of the Serbs, is currently being exercised against the Serbian minority at the hands of the Kosovars. It would be difficult to argue that, as a result of the intervention, democracy has in this region made any great step forward.

The Iraq war

The phrase 'the right to intervene' was not used in the course of the next display of the new political messianism, namely the war in Iraq, led by a coalition of countries under the United States which again went ahead without a resolution from the UN. The pretext for this operation in 2003, later revealed to be entirely fallacious, was the supposed presence in Iraq of 'weapons of mass destruction'. Nevertheless, the spirit of intervening in a good cause was very much in evidence. We find traces of it in a paper outlining the military doctrine of the United States, published by the White House, then under the presidency of George W. Bush, a few months before the invasion, entitled *The National Security Strategy of the United States of America*.

It first identifies various core values, 'freedom, democracy, and free enterprise', and the US government declares that it has a mission: to impose these values right across the surface of the globe, if necessary by force. By winning the victory, it will transform the fate of men for the better. 'Today, humanity holds in its hands the opportunity to further freedom's triumph over all these foes. The United States welcomes our responsibility to lead in this great mission.' The conclusions drawn from the document are clear: 'We will actively work', it says, 'to bring the hope of democracy, development, free markets, and free trade to every corner of the world.' Once again, the noble end justifies the use of any means, including war.

While pursuing lofty ideals, this programme is alarming. It revives the earlier forms of political messianism, Communist promises and colonial projects, which promoted the alluring prospect of the arrival of freedom and equality, fraternity and dignity, while at the same time engaging in military action. It even recalls the older endeavours to conquer in the name of the good that invoked a quasi-religious justification, such as the crusades of the Middle Ages – and the term 'crusade' was actually re-used on this occasion. Each time, the protagonists of these acts might well be sincerely convinced of the superiority of their cause, but this did not stop them bringing blood and tears to the rest of the world.

Why is it dangerous to impose the good? Even assuming that we knew the nature of the latter, we would have to declare war on all those who do not share the same ideal, and there are likely to be a great number of them. As Charles Péguy wrote in the early twentieth century: 'There is in the Declaration of Human Rights enough to make war on everybody for as long as the world lasts!'[18] Countless victims would be required to achieve a bright future. But the nature of this ideal also raises a problem. Is it enough to say 'freedom' for us all to agree what this involves? Do we not know that the tyrants of the past regularly claimed to be acting in the name of freedom? Can we also proclaim, as does the US presidential document (ignoring millennia of human history), 'These values of freedom are right and true for every person, in every society'? Are we really *for* all freedom, unconditionally, including, as they say, the freedom of the fox to gain access to the henhouse? And what is 'free enterprise' doing among the universal values: should we make war on all countries where the economy is run by the state? As for 'democracy' and the equal dignity of all members of the human race, are we still practising this when we stop other people choosing their own destiny for themselves?

Believing that one has been entrusted (by oneself) with a 'mission' that consists in enabling 'freedom to triumph over its enemies' reflects a strange worldview, which, incidentally, does not correspond either to the

Christian tradition or to that of secular humanism. Both of these, in fact, postulate the irreducible imperfection of the human world and the impossibility in principle of attaining any triumph; only millenarian heresies and revolutionary utopias maintained such a hope. 'Freedom' will never finally triumph over its 'foes': it is the human being himself who restrains his impulses towards freedom, and he is right to do so; to produce that other world, we would first need to change our species. It should be added that the messianic ambition of bringing about a harmonious world order emerged, after a while, as a mere rhetorical weapon that did not lead to any practical effects. It was replaced by a no less messianic vision, albeit national in scope rather than universal: that of imposing the will of the United States on the rest of the world.

The occupation of Iraq, begun in 2003, lasted until 2011 and was the longest war in the history of the United States. Meanwhile one dictatorship, that of Saddam Hussein, fell – but at what price? The victims, of whom there were very many, were unevenly distributed between the two belligerents, with about 4,500 killed on the US side; for the Iraqi side, we do not have a precise number, but a plausible figure is 450,000 people, a ratio of 100 to 1 (other calculations give a figure of two or three times as many). The country remains plagued by terrorist attacks and tensions between communities. The idea of preventive war, launched simply on the basis of the assumption of a possible attack from a foreign country, has made its appearance in the official discourse of democratic nations.[19]

The internal damage: torture

The US military severely compromised itself in the management of the occupation, as it made torture in

Iraqi prisons widespread. Abu Ghraib became famous worldwide after the release, in 2004, of photographs showing Iraqi prisoners being tortured; but other similar prisons existed, in Iraq and elsewhere. Subsequent investigations have confirmed the extension of these practices and their systematic nature. Thus, an official publication of the US government, dated April 2009, revealed the incredibly detailed regulation of torture set out in the manual of the CIA and endorsed by the judicial representatives of the government. For this is the novelty: torture is not represented as a regrettable but excusable deviation from the norm: it *is* the norm. Until then, it was possible to imagine that torture was a blunder, as they called it, an unintended overstepping of the limit caused by the urgency of the moment. But instead, people realized that it consisted of procedures set down in the finest detail, to the precise centimetre and the precise second.

Thus, there are ten forms of torture employed, a figure that later rises to thirteen. They are divided into three categories, each of which has several degrees of intensity: preparatory (nakedness, force feeding, sleep deprivation), corrective (blows) and coercive (hosing with water, confinement in boxes, water-boarding). When slapping, the interrogator must hit with his fingers spread, halfway between the point of the chin and the bottom of the earlobe. Hosing a naked prisoner can take twenty minutes if the water is at 5 degrees, forty if it is 10 degrees, and up to sixty if it is 15 degrees. Sleep deprivation must not exceed one hundred and eighty hours, but after eight hours' rest, it can begin again. In water-boarding, immersion can last up to twelve seconds, no more than two hours per day for thirty consecutive days (one particularly tough prisoner suffered this torture 183 times in March 2003). Enclosure in a small box should not exceed two hours, but if the box allows the prisoner to stand up, this measure can be imposed for up to eight hours in succession, eighteen hours a day. If you put an insect in the box, you must not tell the prisoner that its bite will be very painful, even deadly. And so on and so forth, page after page.

The contagion spreads far beyond the limited circle of the torturers: several other groups of professionals are involved in the practice of torture. Legal advisors from the government are available to ensure the legal impunity of their colleagues and provide legitimacy for their actions. Others regularly present include psychologists, psychiatrists, doctors, women (the torturers are men, but degradation in the sight of women compounds the humiliation). Meanwhile, university professors produce moral, legal and philosophical justification for torture. Torture indelibly marks the tortured body, but it also corrupts the minds of the torturers. Gradually, the whole society is affected by this insidious cancer that erodes the fundamental pact linking the citizens of every democratic country, a pact in which the state is the guarantor of justice and respect for every human being. A state that legalizes torture is no longer a democracy.

Such practices, which seem to go against not only the laws of any country but also against widely shared human emotions such as compassion, are easier to accept in times of war than in times of peace, because war always entails the suspension of certain legal and moral norms. The most reprehensible of all actions, killing one's fellow, needs only be renamed 'eliminating an enemy' to become the most valorous of actions. The foundations of common life are shaken, and the transgressions of particular rules cease to appear as such. The war situation has a decisive influence from another point of view: it is universally accepted that in wartime, subordinates owe absolute obedience to their superiors. Faced with the danger of death, with bombs exploding at your side, you have no time for discussions and prevarications. Even in a country that worships free initiative, the circumstances of war require one to obey orders without thinking. We can see how the idea of a 'war against terrorism' can have pernicious effects.

Several analysts have noted the rise of hubris, or excess, among the heads of state who started the war and commanded the armies: American president George W. Bush and British prime minister Tony Blair.[20] But we need to go beyond individual cases: it is not only those individuals who are prey to hubris, but the states themselves which, no longer held back by any external brake, communicate this excess to their leaders. At the end of this path, torture lies. We might add that neither of these leaders of the Iraq campaign has expressed the slightest regret for launching this war; apparently, they are still convinced that they saved the world from disaster.

Democratic values, brandished by the Western countries as a reason for the intervention, were perceived by the people of other countries as a convenient camouflage for nefarious intentions. The erosion of these values, the effect of a messianic impulse towards perfection, can also be found outside of situations of war. The desire to avoid any risk to our health can lead to a utopian version of preventive healthcare; the desire to avoid any social risk, to a policy excluding all potential troublemakers. One of the most powerful threats to our democracy, writes one judge, Serge Portelli, 'is that of a society of absolute security, zero tolerance, radical prevention, preventive confinement, systematic distrust of the foreign, surveillance and generalized control'.[21] Thus we become our own worst enemy – indeed, the worst enemy imaginable.

The war in Afghanistan

The occupation of Afghanistan by the American army and its allies was a consequence of the attacks of 11

September 2001, led by terrorists based in Afghanistan. In the wake of the attack, an intervention by Afghan forces, backed by US soldiers, eliminated al-Qaeda fighters from Afghanistan, and removed the Taliban who were protecting them. The dismay aroused by these terrorist attacks meant that this intervention could be viewed as an act of self-defence. However, without much thought for the consequences of what they were doing, American soldiers, supported by their allies, settled in the country to support the government they had helped to put in place to ensure that no new terrorists would appear. This last objective was in line with the logic of political messianism: the aim was to transform the country into a democracy respectful of human rights. But from this moment, the presence of the military occupation produced the opposite result to what was expected: the more the military personnel reinforced their armed might, the more unanimously were people against them. In other words, the aim proposed by the Americans for their intervention in Afghanistan (i.e. the security of the US) was not achieved by the means chosen (the occupation of a foreign country). In fact, quite the opposite seemed to happen.

Let us look more closely at these two levels of failure. On site, the American soldiers and their auxiliaries are attacked by those they prevent going about their business; in this hostile environment, in an unfamiliar land where every road can be mined and where behind every bush an enemy can be hiding, the occupiers retaliate by shelling. To avoid the risk of dying, they consent to the risk of killing innocent people: in fact, there are always civilians near the fighters they are pursuing. The result is that the enemy continues to grow in number. 'Merely killing insurgents usually serves to multiply enemies rather than subtract them', wrote General Michael T. Flynn in 2010, in a report aimed at improving the situation.[22] Whenever one person is killed, four others take his place – cousins, friends or neighbours.

The general therefore condemns this practice – in the name of efficiency, not humanity. On the other hand, it is a mere oversimplification when the Western press labels all those who oppose the occupation as 'Taliban'. In reality, the opponents form a heterogeneous group combining religious Taliban, local warlords, traffickers of all kinds, producers and distributors of poppies, and conservatives who risk losing their privileges in a Western-style democracy. The unity of the insurgents lies solely in the existence of a common enemy, namely the foreign army of occupation.

The Western audience focuses on the stated objectives of the occupation: supporting democracy, defending human rights, hunting down terrorists. The Afghan people focuses on the reality: the indiscriminate bombings, the detention and torture centres (such as Bagram, the prototype for Abu Ghraib), the support given to corrupt leaders. Should we be surprised that the Afghans do not feel very favourably inclined towards the occupiers? One example among many: in August 2008, a French detachment fell into an ambush, which killed ten soldiers. Such an operation could not be mounted without being known to the local population; yet no one warned the French of the danger. In the days following the ambush on the French, an air raid caused the death of ninety-two civilians, mostly children. How could the occupiers responsible for these deaths expect to be loved and protected by the population?

The presence of an occupying army is not only ineffective, it is harmful to the security of Westerners. The main threat to them comes not from armed Afghan peasants, but from all those who, outside of Afghanistan, feel solidarity with its people for political, religious or cultural reasons. The terrorist of today is not carrying out instructions from an underground central command; sensitive to the humiliation endured by those to whom he feels close, he acts on their behalf of his own free will. Seeking to eliminate some al-Qaeda control centre issuing all the orders for terrorist acts is either pure fantasy, or the application of an outdated model to a new situation. The mountains of Afghanistan (or other countries) do not play a role comparable to that of KGB back rooms in Moscow during the Cold War. The current context is different, marked by technological change and globalization. There is much *talk* in the West of the danger Islam represents for countries in Europe or North America, but what we *see* are Western armies occupying Muslim countries or intervening in them by force of arms. This fact is abundantly exploited by the propaganda of the enemies of the West, a propaganda spread today by the Internet and immediately able to reach a wider audience.

To combat terrorism effectively, Westerners have two methods at their disposal, neither of them military. They can resort to policing (informing, monitoring, controlling financial circuits); or they can use political methods (avoiding the accusation that the values defended are merely a pretext for occupation). Today the occupation of Afghanistan has become a cause of aggression, instead of being a remedy against it. At the same time, this military commitment comes at such a high price that it should shock the populations of Western countries, especially in these times of economic and financial crisis. If this does not happen, it is because such colossal sums can no longer be imagined. Before the election of Barack Obama as American president, the war in Afghanistan had already cost $1 trillion ($1,000 billion); it has since swallowed up $1 billion a week. The increased commitment of 2010 meant an additional $30 billion. The allies are also called on to contribute: the war costs France €1 million per day. Is this really the best use of that money?

The temptations of pride and power

These arguments against American military involvement
in Afghanistan, already expressed by various commentators, must be known to Obama, a self-declared
opponent of the Iraq war when it was initiated by
President Bush. Nor can he be unaware of the fragility of the view that this intervention is a 'just war'. In
his speech in Oslo, where he went to receive the Nobel
Peace Prize in December 2009, Obama declared that the
United States was waging a 'just war' in Afghanistan
and listed three conditions, all necessary for a war to
be declared 'just': 'if it is waged as a last resort or in
self-defense; if the force used is proportional; and if,
whenever possible, civilians are spared from violence'.
But none of these three conditions is satisfied in the present circumstances: no one, in Afghanistan or elsewhere,
can seriously believe that the local warlords or religious
fighters threaten the security of the United States; no
one can deem an army of 100,000 men against 500
al-Qaeda fighters to be 'proportional'; and nobody can
deny that air strikes entail significant civilian casualties.
So why persist in getting bogged down in a path that
does not lead to the desired goal?

The only rational answer is that the aim pursued is
not the stated purpose. We can get an idea of the first
aim from a few sentences that Obama let slip in the
same speech. The United States, he says, is required to
carry a 'burden' – no longer that of the white man, as
in Kipling, but of a people charged with a special mission: helping to 'underwrite global security', in other
words being the police force for mankind and contrib-
uting to the promotion of freedom around the world.
This would be in the 'enlightened self-interest' of the
American people. The political messianism that had led
to the Iraq war is still alive. But it is based on a collective belief which, though not religious in origin, has the

same absolute character as a divine commandment and seems to elude rational argumentation. Otherwise, what could be the origin of such a mission?

In the same vein, Obama openly considers the usefulness of war 'beyond self-defense or the defense of one nation against an aggressor', such as protecting a population against its own government, or stopping a civil war; in short, 'I believe that force can be justified on humanitarian grounds.' Such interventions, he says, can be carried out as a preventive measure. It is at this point that American policy tips over from the universal principle of the right to self-defence into the messianism which leads the US to believe it has the task of saving humanity. Obama thinks it is necessary to assure us that 'Evil does exist in the world.' True, but should we not insist, rather, on the fact that the temptation of good (what he himself calls 'the temptations of pride, and power') has wrought infinitely more damage than the 'temptation of evil'? If we resign ourselves to imposing the good by force, we have abandoned the principle to which Obama at the same time appeals, namely that all people are motivated by the same basic needs and therefore deserve the same respect; instead, some people now decide on others' behalf. Finally, if the notion of a 'just war' might meet with some reservations, that of a 'humanitarian war' makes us think quite simply of Orwell and the slogans of the Party in *1984*.

Waging this war is apparently considered to be in the interests of the American people, because it proves and illustrates its military superiority (we know that this superiority is undeniable, and that the United States is ready to pay the price: its military budget, $600 billion a year, is equal to the sum of the military budgets of all countries of the rest of the world put together). The desire for power does not need any justification beyond power itself. Other reasons may exist from time to time (for example, ensuring the strategic oil supply), but overall, we seek power for power's sake. It is essential to avoid losing face, on this view; any acknowledgement that the campaign in Afghanistan was unjustified would inevitably have a negative effect. Obama therefore prefers to legitimize the present error by a past error.

The war in Libya: the decision

The latest of the Western interventions meant to bring the good to the other countries in the world was the Libyan war, launched in March 2011 and won by August of the same year. One apparent difference between this war and those that preceded it, in Iraq and Afghanistan, was that this time there *was* a resolution of the Security Council of the UN authorizing the intervention. In addition, this resolution was justified by a new principle, summarized by the phrase the 'responsibility to protect'. However, despite appearances, and despite the solemn invocations of the noble principles of freedom, democracy, human rights and respect for the people, the situation was not all that different. Let us first examine these two innovations.

The 'responsibility to protect' is a concept born of an observed fact – the terrible impotence of the United Nations at the time of the Rwandan genocide. I have mentioned the invocation, on that occasion, of a 'right to intervene' militarily in emergency situations; but the formula did not inspire confidence among people in the rest of the world, as it was a little too reminiscent of the earlier era in which the great powers decided among themselves on the course the affairs of the world should take. The 'responsibility to protect' appeared to be a more cautious formulation, and the principle was adopted by a vote of the General Assembly of the UN in 2005. The underlying idea was that if a government lacks the capacity or willingness to protect its civilian population, the United Nations has the right to intervene in this country without seeking government approval. Colonel Gaddafi had ordered the bloody repression of those who demanded his departure, so the principle of protection seemed to apply.

But the truth of the matter is that the meaning of the decision is not entirely clear. First, the formula is itself vague. Should we understand it in a minimalist sense, as the introduction of humanitarian aid? Or admit that this aid should be protected by a military force? Or interpret it as the destruction of any armed forces that threaten the civilian population? Or should we follow a maximalist interpretation, and view it as the overthrow of the government held responsible for this situation, and its replacement by another viewed as preferable by those intervening? Depending on the way we answer these questions, we obviously end up in very different situations. And once this 'protection' no longer means just humanitarian assistance, but the military intervention of another state, it is unclear how it differs from the 'right to intervene' appealed to previously.

In addition, the interpretation and application of this 'responsibility' are entrusted to the Security Council of the UN, where, of course, the permanent members (the United States, Russia, China, Britain and France) have a right of veto. This particular arrangement is the original sin of the Council and thus of the international order that it is supposed to guarantee. By giving themselves this right, the permanent members of the Council immediately set themselves above the law they are supposed to implement: neither they nor the countries they choose to protect can be condemned. So the justice in question is highly selective. This helps explain why, despite the proven suffering of the civilian populations, some interventions will never take place. Just think of the Chechens in Russia, the Tibetans in China, the Shiites in Sunni countries (and vice versa), the Palestinians in the territories occupied by Israel, and so on. Just as intervention in Libya was being decided on, the members of the Council were encouraging the very different intervention of Saudi Arabia in its neighbouring countries, in defence of the government in power against mass rebellion. And, citing the need for a local balance, the Council was also content merely to reprimand Syria for the similar repression it was practising against its own population.

The situation is actually even worse: the permanent members may decide to intervene wherever they want to *without* the authorization of the United Nations, as they did in Kosovo and Iraq; it is clear that this does not entail any official sanction. The international order embodied by the Security Council establishes the rule of force, not of law. It is sometimes said, with a touch of pride, that this new world order has brought to an end the sacrosanct Westphalian notion of the sovereignty of states, the principle that each government does what it wants at home, and can decide on what is right or wrong. Though this order is certainly imperfect, it has been replaced by an even older order based on the idea that might is right and that the powerful of this world can impose their will on the weaker.

Subjecting the principle of national sovereignty to universal governance is an act which by itself creates inequality, since the world is now divided into two groups of states, those that can do what they want at home and abroad (the permanent members of the Security Council, which have a right of veto) and those that, like the weak-minded, or like young children, are under the supervision of the former and will be punished for any transgression of the rules. That is why international life has preferred, at other times in its history, to follow a different principle: not the imposition of the same good on all, but the acceptance of the plurality of ideals and the sovereignty of countries. It is, indeed, still the only principle compatible with the idea of equality between countries, as opposed to dividing them into two categories: those who deserve to rule themselves, and those who need to be governed by others, as in colonial times. When today we see the newspaper headlines proclaiming that 'The fate of Libya is being decided in London and Paris', we might think we had gone back one hundred and thirty years, to when Britain and France, the great colonial powers, effectively ruled Africa and Asia and chose the rulers of the country under their tutelage.

The war in Libya: the implementation

The first victim of the intervention, even before the bombs meant to protect the population started falling, was the political and media discourse in the countries which had taken the initiative: any desire for precision and nuance was forgotten, leaving instead Manichaean simplifications, antithetical superlatives, fudged approximations, and hymns to victory. The enemy leader was referred to only in invective, he had become insane, crazy, an executioner, a bloody or sinister tyrant, or simply reduced to his roots as a 'cunning Bedouin'. Opposite him were lined up the white knights bringing freedom, the peerless soldiers defending universal values. Patriots crowed aloud: France should be rightly proud of her role in the war, she had brought off a great feat by having been the first to commit her forces, she had defended her honour. The war was beautiful, the victories would enter legend. Euphemisms were commonplace: it was not said that we should kill without remorse, but that 'we must assume our responsibilities'; we should not keep the number of dead low, but we must proceed 'without causing undue damage'. Dodgy comparisons justified France's going to war: not to intervene would repeat the mistakes made in Spain in

1937, in Munich in 1938, Rwanda in 1994 . . . Airdrops
of weapons to insurgents reminded President Sarkozy of
those dropped by British airmen for resistance fighters
in France during World War II.

When we go beyond this euphoric rhetoric, we find a
slightly different reality. The initial goal was to loosen
the stranglehold of Gaddafi's army, which threatened to
cause a bloodbath in Benghazi. This goal, which could
be judged in itself legitimate, was reached on the first
day. The realization soon hit home: the real purpose of
the foreign states involved in the war was not just the
protection of the civilian population – or rather, this
protection was to be interpreted in a very broad sense.
The aim of the operation was to remove the head of the
state and replace him with another, more benevolent
towards the West, or more docile. The resolution of
the Security Council was passed on 17 February, the
intervention began on 19 March: on 24 February, the
French defence minister Alain Juppé said that Gaddafi
must leave power; the next day, the French president
confirmed as much. A little later, the new defence minister, Gérard Longuet, explained that the two objectives
needed to be united: 'The protection of populations
involved striking at the whole chain of command.'

The purpose of the intervention had never really been
to impose a ceasefire, as demands on this issue were
only unilateral: the loyalists were asked to suspend their
attacks, but the insurgents were not required to lay
down their weapons. Moreover, the latter were hostile
to the idea of a ceasefire: they preferred that the fight
should continue until NATO had destroyed or driven
out their opponents. This explains why the NATO
bombing was soon concentrated not on the cities
besieged by the loyalists, but on the capital, Tripoli.
Officially, the elimination of Gaddafi was not part of
the objectives, but the Alliance took care to bomb all the
places where he might be, all the centres of command,

control and communication; if he were killed, it would not be, so to speak, on purpose . . .

In fact, the initial situation, when a crowd demonstrating peacefully was brutally repressed by the regime's forces, quickly turned into a civil war between supporters and opponents of Gaddafi, loyalists and rebels, backed by the various tribes that make up this nation. NATO therefore put itself at the service of one of the factions in the civil war. From this point of view, the situation resembled that of Kosovo in 1999 when NATO led the war against the Serbian authorities instead of the UCK, the Albanian-speaking insurgent group. The Libyan war caused, on the reckoning of the chairman of the National Transitional Council (NTC), Mustafa Abdul Jalil, about 20,000 deaths, a figure raised to 30,000 in October. The victims of NATO bombing formed a proportion of this, though we do not know exactly how many. We will not here consider the fallacious distinction proposed by the International Criminal Court between deliberately targeted victims (those of Gaddafi) and victims killed unintentionally (those of NATO): bombs are designed to destroy and kill. What happens is that the enemy victims are simply not included in the count. Among the 'collateral damage' we must also mention the refugees fleeing a war-torn country, crammed into makeshift boats, telling themselves that their neighbour, Europe, would open her arms wide to welcome them. The number of deaths by drowning off the Libyan coast is estimated at 1,200.

NATO's commitment was decisive for the outcome of the fighting. At the beginning of the conflict, the loyalists were better armed than the insurgents, so they managed to win a few local victories. However, very quickly, this initial imbalance between the insurgent forces and those of the loyalists was reversed: the cannons of the insurgents destroyed the guns of the loyalists, just as the missiles of NATO easily annihilated the cannons of the loyalist army. Given this disproportion between forces, the military outcome of the confrontation was not in doubt, and the only unknown variable was how long each battle would last. The action began with the control of air space (destruction of enemy aircraft and air defences). NATO alone, which took command of operations on 31 March, carried out 20,262 sorties, of which 7,635 resulted in strikes. It also seized control of the sea, with sixteen naval vessels. Through targeted raids, it cut off the loyalists' oil supply and also provided the insurgents with weapons. The capture of Tripoli was made possible by the close cooperation between the insurgents and NATO: over three days, the latter bombed forty-two targets in the city, including Gaddafi's fortress-residence, and also carried out drone strikes and placed 'technicians' to help out on the ground. It was French planes which, in October 2011, made the capture and lynching of Gaddafi possible. Unsurprisingly, bombs had the last word: we had won.

The ambiguity over the objective of the intervention raised many questions and aroused some resistance, which increased gradually as the end approached. The intervention met with initial disapproval from the countries of the African Union, and then gradually from the BRICS countries (Brazil, Russia, India, China, South Africa) which had abstained in the Security Council vote and which alone account for the majority of the world's population: they declared that the NATO campaign was going far beyond what had been authorized by this resolution. 'Instead of protecting people,' said South African president Jacob Zuma, the 'intervention has allowed the rebel group to make progress.' In Europe itself, it did not gain majority support: only Italy, Denmark, Norway and Belgium joined the leading combatant countries, Great Britain and France.

The West had chosen to call Gaddafi's supporters 'mercenaries' or 'subject populations', and his enemies 'the people' – and then chose to support the latter. It also bestowed the description 'democrats' on them, though there was nothing to justify this. From what we know today, the forces hostile to Gaddafi were extremely heterogeneous. They did include defenders of democratic ideas, but also Islamists and al-Qaeda fighters, former officials of the Gaddafi regime and Libyans who had emigrated to the West and established strong links with political and business circles. To take a few examples, the president of the CNT, Abdul Jalil, was for years the head of the Court of Appeal of Tripoli; as such, he twice confirmed the death sentences of the Bulgarian nurses accused of spreading AIDS in Libya. As a reward for his good services, Gaddafi appointed him minister of justice, a position he retained until his defection in February 2011.

The armed forces of the rebels were commanded for a time by General Abdul Fatah Younis, a comrade of Gaddafi from 1969 to 2011, a former interior minister and head of the special troops responsible for decades of repression. He was killed in unclear circumstances at the end of July 2011, probably by former Islamists: previously, he had been responsible for hunting them down. The new military governor of Tripoli was Abdelhakim Belhaj, a former member of al-Qaeda, a fighter in Afghanistan, detained and tortured by the CIA before being handed over to Libyan captors. The great protector of the insurgents, the emir of Qatar, is not particularly known for his democratic aspirations. As for the 'prime minister' of the NTC, Mahmoud Jibril, and his 'Mr Oil', Ali Tarhouni, they are best known for having studied and worked extensively in the United States. Is not all the 'democratic' discourse of the Western countries a bit misplaced in the context of Libya, a country that has never had an election, and that has no political parties or any equivalent of what is called 'civil society'?

Idealists and realists

Noting that the 'democratic' argument is not enough to explain why the West chose one of the belligerents rather than the other, we may wonder if it would not be closer to the truth to see the initial revolt as a coup whose leaders offered the West a deal: the NATO forces would eliminate Gaddafi so they could seize power, in exchange for which they would give their benefactors free access to the country's oil reserves . . . This strategy seems particularly probable, as having a faithful ally in Tripoli can be quite useful at a time when the political upheavals in neighbouring Arab countries might bring to power leaders less favourably disposed towards the West than the vanquished autocrats.

This hypothesis received early confirmation in the days that followed the fall of Tripoli: the press published a letter from the CNT, dating back several months, which promised to earmark 35 per cent of its oil production for France as a reward for 'total and permanent support of our Council'. The letter was repudiated by the leaders of the CNT, but in terms that are worth noting. Thus Abdul Jalil, on 25 August: 'We promise to favour the countries which helped us, we will treat them according to the support they have given us.' French minister Alain Juppé recorded the message: 'It seems quite logical and fair to me', he agreed. At the same time, the French defence minister reported that France was responsible for 35 per cent of the air strikes on Gaddafi's forces, a curious coincidence of numbers. If this relationship is confirmed, we can say that the humanitarian cause (preventing bloodshed) was a kind of Trojan horse, a good excuse to intervene militarily and control the political orientation of a state rich in energy reserves.

There are certainly many reasons why this intervention was carried out even though, in very similar circumstances, others were not: why Libya and not

Syria, or Bahrain, or Yemen? These reasons may be related to difficulties experienced by the leaders of the intervening states at a particular point in their careers, or the political and economic interests of these states. France continued for a long time to support dictatorships established in the neighbouring countries, Tunisia and Egypt; by choosing to back the insurgents in Libya, she could hope to be following the flow of history. She was at the same time demonstrating the effectiveness of her weapons, which put her in a strong position in future negotiations. But over and above individual justifications, a common framework was also being maintained.

In his speech of 28 March 2011, President Obama provided the intervention with an overall legitimation rather similar to the one he had previously given to the Afghanistan war. Well aware that the security of the United States was not at stake in Libya (this was not a war of self-defence), he relied on the exceptional role that falls to his country in the maintenance of the international order. 'The United States of America has played a unique role as an anchor of global security and as an advocate for human freedom', and has a responsibility to give the lead to the rest of the world. It must intervene whenever, in some corner of the world, a natural disaster occurs, but also 'preventing genocide and keeping the peace; ensuring regional security, and maintaining the flow of commerce' (clearly, the economic interests of the United States are no more forgotten by Obama than they were by George W. Bush). The nature of this mission is now specified: it is neither divine, nor the result of a consensus, but simply follows from the US's status as 'the world's most powerful nation'. This is how might is enabled to pass itself off as right! And Obama concluded, applying the theory to this particular case: Gaddafi must relinquish power.

The intervention in Libya confirms the messianic

pattern familiar to Western democracies. Because of their technological, economic and military success, they are convinced of their moral and political superiority over the other countries in the world. So they decide that their military power gives them the right or even the duty to manage the affairs of the world (excluding the other permanent members of the Security Council and their protégés), by imposing on countries that fail to meet their requirements the values judged to be superior and, in practice, giving them governments deemed capable of conducting the appropriate policy. The case of Britain and France, which dominated the coalition engaged on action in Libya, is a little more specific. These two countries were the major colonial powers one hundred or two hundred years ago, though they have now become middle-ranking powers that need to bear in mind the desires of stronger countries. But here they were offered an opportunity to show their military capabilities and enjoy the feeling that they could again manage the affairs of the world; they willingly seized their chance. Encouraged by the results, the French president soon designated the next target: on 31 August 2011, he warned Iran of the possibility of a 'pre-emptive strike' against its nuclear sites, so endorsing the notion of preventive war put forward by George W. Bush.

A different outcome to the Libyan crisis could have been imagined, one which was requested by other African countries – but their opinion was considered negligible. After the initial response that destroyed the air forces of the regime and stopped the government troops' advance towards the cities in the hands of the insurgents, it would have been possible to impose a ceasefire on all belligerents. After this, political talks could have been started, preferably under the auspices of the African Union. Gaddafi's departure could have been negotiated under these conditions; if no agreement was reached, a transformation of the country into a federation, or its partitioning, would have been the answer. These solutions were admittedly tentative and imperfect, but free of the excess behind the idea of imposing the good by force.

For now, the intervention in Libya led by Britain and France with the help of the United States has met with the support of a large part of the population of these countries. The 'liberal hawks', as they are called in the United States, advocates of a muscular interventionism in the name of democratic values and human rights, are in agreement with the nationalist defenders of their countries' interests: Gaddafi was a terrible dictator, and furthermore his country has the largest oil reserves on the continent of Africa. This coincidence explains why left and right can accept such a choice, especially since, thanks to technological superiority, this war did not cause casualties among the populations of the intervening countries. In addition to the supporters of the war are those who like to be on the side of the winners; together, they do indeed form a majority. Yet we may also fear that as the veil of idealism no longer hides realistic interests, the populations of these countries will interpret the whole sequence of events as an eloquent lesson in moral cynicism. The current stigmatization of the Gaddafi regime, indeed, throws a cruel light on the policy of these countries over the past years. From 2004, in fact, his regime was given approval and gestures of friendship, French and British heads of state rubbed shoulders in Tripoli, and even the secret services of both sides willingly exchanged information or, as in the case of Abdelhakim Belhaj, recalcitrant prisoners. So was all this just hypocrisy? How can we then believe in the veracity of public words, how can we have confidence in our political leaders? It is doubtful that this lesson will play a useful part in the proper civic education of the people.

You could also say that, in general, the relations

between nations obey force and material interests alone, unlike the relations established within each nation. In this case, what is the point of waxing indignant at each new example of this law? But, assuming that things are like this, how can we not see that the victims – collateral, if you will, and yet inevitable – will be the very ideas of justice, democracy and human rights, now appearing as a convenient camouflage for actions meant to provide us with greater wealth and power? Would it not be better to remove the 'gift wrap' in which intervention is presented and get a little closer to the truth? Let us not forget at the same time that those who suffer our 'humanitarian wars' do not suffer any less than victims of the old-style wars. Before singing a hymn to the glory of a new, greatly improved conflagration, we might do better to ponder the lessons that Goya drew, two hundred years ago, from another war conducted in the name of the good, when Napoleon's regiments brought freedom and progress to the Spaniards. The massacres committed in the name of democracy are no easier to live with than those brought about by faith in God or Allah, the Guide or the Party. They all lead to the same 'Disasters of War' memorialized by Goya.

Politics in the face of morality and justice

The third phase of political messianism is a paradoxical effect of the happy event which closed the history of the twentieth century: the fall of the Berlin Wall, the collapse of Communist regimes, the end of the totalitarian episode. Previously, the balance between the two superpowers – a balance of terror – had ensured the relative stability of the world; each of them could 'clean up' in its sphere of influence and dominate its satellites, but each also acted as a brake on the other. Since then, there has been only a single superpower, and the danger of excess has appeared in a new form, since there is nothing to stop it doing what it wants. The United States is tempted to become the planetary policeman, to impose its will by force – a will presented, to nobody's surprise, as the good.

The proponents of this strategy are recruited from across the current political spectrum, left and right. The intervention in Kosovo occurred under President Bill Clinton, the one in Iraq under George W. Bush, the wars in Afghanistan and Libya under Barack Obama: the superior interests of state seem to trump, every time, the particular views or intentions of the American president. It is as if the head of the most powerful country in the world could not do otherwise. All things considered, the same could be said of European leaders, the political class as a whole or its intellectuals: they are recruited equally from all political families.

In the course of history, many military interventions have assumed this almost moral stance, but they seem to characterize Western political messianism more particularly. The pattern is the same: when action is taken, its universal and moral scope is announced – it is a matter of improving the lot of the whole or part of mankind – and this unleashes a wave of enthusiasm, thereby facilitating the project. We are convinced that, by a simple effect of collective will, we can achieve any goal and move forward indefinitely along the path of progress. Sometime later – a year, a century – we see that the supposedly universal goal was not what it seemed, but corresponded rather to the interests of those who had formulated it. So we swear we will never fall into the same trap again – unless the new circumstances are truly exceptional . . .

The practical effect of these endeavours is, all in all, negative. Beyond specific cases, we can point to two structural reasons for this.

The first is that the violence of the means cancels out

the nobility of the ends. There are no humanitarian bombs or merciful wars: the populations who suffer them count the bodies and have no time for the sublime objectives (dignity! freedom! human rights! civilization!). The proponents of these interventions discover, to their surprise, that they produce the opposite effect to the aims pursued. Their failure stems from the fact that they have chosen to act *either* from their convictions alone, without worrying about the consequences of their acts, *or* just from a need to win an immediate success, regardless of the moral and legal framework within which these acts fall. The ethics of conviction spoken of by Max Weber is not opposed to the ethics of responsibility, but to pure pragmatism, to the quest for direct effectiveness. Responsibility, however, implies both that we find a moral and legal basis for the policy we are pursuing, and that we take into account all the aspects of the context, including the likely effects of its action, without which the whole endeavour is doomed to failure.

The second reason is that, since we have to impose good on others by force, instead of just offering it to them, we assume at the outset that they are incapable of managing themselves and that, in order to be freed, they must first submit. But to suppose that there is this inequality between them and us goes against the first principle of justice and morality, and against what we were supposedly representing. The result of this internal contradiction is that the democratic values that we claimed to serve are permanently compromised, since they appear to their intended beneficiaries as a mask for other motivations – political, economic or ideological. It also compromises humanitarian actions carried out by the same countries even though these can indeed be disinterested. This compromising of humanitarian workers becomes inevitable when they accept the logistical support provided by the army of occupation, or when, publicly referring to transgressions of human rights, they contribute to the unleashing of military action.

Note that it is not human rights themselves that are in question here, but how we seek to promote them: rather than being a personal ideal, or a horizon of actions undertaken by civil society, or a basis for legislation in democratic countries, they are presented as the operational principle of a state's foreign policy, thereby lending legitimacy to wars whose aim is the establishment of the good. Observing the harm of this type of invocation of universal values and morality in international relations does not mean renouncing them in principle, but suggests that we should limit their presence to specific situations, depending on an ever-changing context. We cannot prevent war; but, even in time of war, we can, in the name of these values, banish torture or rape or enslavement. In an extreme case, such as genocide occurring in a neighbouring country, an unsolicited military intervention is conceivable – but it must be remembered that, precisely because the mention of genocide arouses strong reactions, the word can be used as a means of manipulation, to achieve other goals. While the word has been frequently bandied around, there was no genocide in Kosovo in 1999, any more than there was in Darfur in 2009. There has, in recent years, been a worrying trivialization of the term: judging by the frequency with which it is used, you would think that, in the entire history of mankind, there has never been a period so rich in genocide as that following the end of the Cold War.

Undeniably, there are legitimate wars: wars of self-defence (such as World War II for the Allies, or the US intervention in Afghanistan in 2001), wars that prevent genocide or massacre (the Vietnamese intervention that stopped the genocide in Cambodia in 1978–9 would be one of the few examples). On the other hand, wars that are part of a messianic project and whose justification lies in imposing a higher social order on another country, or in making human rights prevail in it, are not legitimate.

Just as it should not be reduced to the application of moral principles, international politics cannot be subject to the rules of law. The reason is simple: to be effective, justice requires a force that can execute it, and such a force belongs to individual states. As long as there is not a world government – an unattractive prospect! – universal justice is likely to remain a façade that serves the stronger. Since 2002, there has been an International Criminal Court, established according to the Rome Statute. Is this really a step towards universal justice? Allow me to refuse to jump on the bandwagon of enthusiasm. Indeed, the prosecutor of this Court answers directly to the Security Council of the UN, where the five permanent members have, as we have recalled, a veto. International justice reflects this initial inequality. No charge can, in principle, be brought against any one of these countries, or against the allies it wishes to protect. Thus, the bombing of Gaza by Israel, of Georgia by Russia, or of Iraq by the United States will never be condemned by the International Court. The only individuals who so far have been charged come from African countries: Uganda, the Congo, the Central African Republic and Sudan.

We need not comment on the way responsibility is thus shared out; but it is worth recalling a recent example. In March 2011, the trial of Charles Taylor, former president of Liberia, took place in The Hague, at the Special Court for Sierra Leone (a body created by the UN). His lawyers wondered why the other leaders of the civil war that ravaged Sierra Leone, such as heads of state of Libya and Burkina Faso, were not arraigned at the same time. The reason was simple, said the attorney general: the powers that fund the tribunal (the United States and Great Britain) would have refused. Telegrams revealed by WikiLeaks show that the idea of putting Charles Taylor on trial had been advanced by the US Embassy in Liberia in order to discredit the country's leader. Taylor very probably does have blood on his hands, but this bad reputation is not the only reason for his indictment; other reasons are involved too, such as political arguments proper to the governments of the most powerful countries, and even the private groups that influence their decisions.[23]

In May 2011, there were two other demonstrations of international justice. While French and British planes were bombing Tripoli, the prosecutor of this Court requested that the Libyan leader and some of his associates be put on trial for crimes against humanity. Can we really trust the impartiality of this system of justice which obeys the instructions of the very Security Council that was responsible for the intervention in Libya? Are the civilian victims of some conflicts more valuable than those of others? Does not this decision look more like a transformation of the justice system into a henchman of NATO, as had already happened in 1999, during the war against Serbia?

At the same time, it was announced that the Serbian general Ratko Mladić, held responsible for the Srebrenica massacres in Bosnia in 1994, had been arrested and transferred to the International Court in The Hague, charged with crimes committed during the war in Yugoslavia. These events were hailed in various places as the sign of significant progress in international justice and as evidence that, gradually, might is everywhere being subjected to right. People took this as an opportunity to say (not for the first time) that, henceforth, all heads of state and senior officials will tremble in fear when they commit despicable acts because they will one day be held accountable. But this picture is an illusion. The only ones threatened are the leaders of weak states without powerful protectors, such as most African countries. Unless some titanic war breaks out, no American, British, French, Russian, Chinese or Indian (etc.) president or warlord will ever be held legally responsible for his actions. International law is still in thrall to force, provided that this force is real.

Morality and justice placed at the service of state policy actually harm morality and justice, turning them into mere tools in the hands of the powerful and making them seem like a hypocritical veil thrown over the defence of their own interests. Messianism, this policy carried out on behalf of the good and the just, does both a disservice. Nothing seems better to illustrate the famous words of Pascal: 'he who would act the angel acts the brute'.[24] International order is not improved when one group of countries is allowed to impose their will without restriction on all others. The temptation of excess then becomes too great and there is a risk of damaging democracy in the eyes of those who should benefit from it, and also eroding its principles among those very people who promote it.

4

The Tyranny of Individuals

Protecting individuals

In the conflict with totalitarianism, democracy faced forces that were posing an obstacle to the freedom of all. This meant a hypertrophy of the collective sphere to the detriment of the individual, with this collective itself being subjected to a small group of tyrannical leaders. But today, in the Western world, one of the main threats to democracy comes not from an excessive expansion of the collective; rather it lies in an unprecedented strengthening of certain individuals, who endanger the well-being of society as a whole.

To observe the rise of this new danger, we again need to go back to the time of the French Revolution, which replaced the power of divine right (based on a law imposed from elsewhere) with the power of the people (who give themselves their own law). This goal was quickly reached; but some perspicacious spirits immediately noticed that the disadvantages of the old order were not entirely overcome. The power of the state was legitimized; but the previous decades had seen the emergence of a new social actor, the individual. And this individual was no better treated by the new regime than by the old; absolutism survived despite the Revolution, and this individual was not protected by law.

Condorcet was one of these lucid spirits. He noted that his contemporaries had a thirst for freedom unknown to their ancestors: the freedom to choose their religion, to seek the truth unhindered, to organize their private lives as they saw fit. A few years later, when Napoleon took power in France, another author powerfully formulated what he called the 'second principle of politics'. This was Benjamin Constant, who in 1806 wrote his great treatise on *The Principles of Politics*. This book was not brought out in its entirety in his lifetime, but Constant did publish various fragments. In one of them, he wrote: 'Sovereignty exists only in a limited and relative way. Where the independence of individual existence begins, the jurisdiction of this sovereignty comes to an end.'[1]

As a result of the disaster unleashed by the Terror, when the sovereign power of the people went so badly astray, Constant and other liberals of the period realized the necessity of isolating and protecting the space of 'individual existence'. So, in their view, the precautions taken by Montesquieu to distinguish between the powers at work in society so that one could limit the other, and the accommodations adopted by European monarchies, in which the temporal power (the state) and the spiritual power (the church) limited each other mutually, were not enough. Liberal thought here introduced a new and different element: the individual, not as a power but as a being to be protected and a value to be cherished. The moderation of the political regime, in other words the pluralism and mutual limitation of powers, was now simply a means designed to lead to this ultimate goal, the protection and flourishing of the individual. Henceforth, the individual was no longer thought within the liberal worldview as being an element of a set (society as a whole), but as an autonomous entity, whose social life was merely one circumstance among others. Depending on whether this social life contributed or not to the well-being of the individual, it was envisaged sometimes as a help, and sometimes as a hindrance.

This raises the question of knowing how far this existence, free of all social control, extends. To begin with, Constant allows only civil liberties. As long as an individual does not harm anyone else, he must be able to remain free to act, to believe what he wants, to express his thoughts, and finally to be treated in accordance with the laws. In a later chapter in his work, however, Constant envisages another type of liberty, situated in the material sphere, and concerning what he calls industry or what we would call the economy. He abandons the idea of 'seeing commercial liberty as equal to civil liberty',[2] as he is aware that the first creates different problems from the second and he does not want any questioning of the former to lead us to doubt the necessity of the latter. However, over the following years, he would increasingly tend to place economic freedom on the same level as other individual freedoms.

In the eighteenth century there occurred what Louis Dumont called 'an unprecedented innovation: the radical separation of the economic aspects of the social fabric and their construction into an autonomous domain'.[3] This separation came to a logical conclusion in Adam Smith's *The Wealth of Nations* (1776), but the ground had been laid by the work of several earlier scholars and philosophers. In traditional societies, economics is just one of several dimensions in the social world; in France and England, in the eighteenth century, people started to think of the economy as a separate activity, different from politics, ethics and religion, an activity that, for this reason, gradually escaped any moral value judgement: the prosperity of the economy became a goal in itself. Constant's specific contribution to this debate resides in the way that he includes the demand for economic autonomy with other civil liberties – and these liberties are one of the main qualities of the democratic society he seeks.

Explaining human behaviour

At the same time, another fundamental shift occurred. Newton's discoveries concerning gravity had a wide impact, and the shadow of the brilliant physicist hovered over the whole eighteenth century. Many philosophers and scholars scrutinized human behaviour and dreamt of discovering laws that would be just as general and objective as those established by Newton for the physical world. Helvétius, author of *On the Mind* (1758), hoped to base morality, like all the other sciences, 'on experiment'.[4] Condorcet, trained as a mathematician, was convinced that all 'human knowledge' could become the object of the 'mathematical sciences' and obtain the same rigour. This was rather begging the question and had little impact on the judicious remarks formulated by the same Condorcet in connection with the differences between the two objects to be known, the material world and human world.

Constant in turn was to follow this path, and this decisively influenced his conception of political action. He was convinced that social life obeyed rigorous laws, and that it was possible to discover them. The revolutionaries, as faithful disciples of Pelagius, believed that human will could transform society and its members in whatever way it wanted (as we saw with Saint-Just). In so doing, thought Constant, they turned their backs on the knowledge of the human world which revealed a completely different truth: the will has only superficial effects, and men are in reality moved by forces which they do not know. These forces are no longer identified, as in the past, with divine design, but with historical and social laws which scholars need to formulate. These unwritten laws, at work in human affairs, are much more important than the artificial and circumstantial laws through which the rulers of each country aim to reform the morals of their citizens. Constant writes:

> As laws are merely the expression of relations between men and these relations are determined by their nature, nobody can create a new law, as this is merely a new declaration of what already existed. [. . .] The legislator is, for the social order, what the physicist is for nature. Newton himself could only observe nature, and tell us of the laws he recognized or thought he recognized.[5]

Once it is assumed that the laws of nature and society have replaced God's designs, we seem much closer to Augustine than to Pelagius.

So human behaviour would seem to have no specific quality to separate it from the movements of the heavenly and earthly bodies. This rejection of any distinction is the logical conclusion of a long development. We find in the Western tradition, whether of Platonic or of Christian origin, a tendency to imagine man as an isolated being who, before coming into contact with his fellows, has relationships solely with non-human things and creatures. Such a vision contrasts with what we find in most other traditions and mythologies in the world, where man is not imagined as existing prior to the social being that we know, and has no relationship to things preceding his relationship to other human beings. At the end of the eighteenth century, Locke translated this Western vision into modern terms: man is the owner of the fruit his labour (in this, he resembles God, the possessor of the world that he has just created in six days), even before he comes into relation with other men, who are here optional mediators.

Locke's eighteenth-century successors tried to interpret relationships between men *as if* they were relationships between men and things, and this made it possible to isolate the economic domain from the rest of social life. There was a twofold advantage to this: the individual affirms his ability (he depends on himself alone) and he is able to gain a good knowledge of the human world, since this is identified with the material world, which, being created by us, is one we can master.[6] Rousseau was part of this tradition and he noted that it was impossible to reduce the social world to the world of nature – a fact that he regretted: 'If the laws of nations, like the laws of nature, could never be broken by any human power, the dependence on men would become dependence on things.'[7] Half a century later, the utopian writer Saint-Simon turned this comparison into one of the fundamental postulates of his scientistic doctrine, claiming that it was necessary *to replace the government of men by the administration of things.*

In Constant, the first consequence of identifying the social with the physical world was that the field of political action shrank considerably. The reformist zeal and the legislative frenzy of the revolutionaries were vain and even harmful. The state's action, thought Constant (and other neoliberals would follow him here), had to be essentially limited to ensuring the security of the citizens, with the aid of justice and the police at home, and of the army when the threat came from outside; it also had to collect the taxes necessary to maintain these services. Otherwise, the state was to leave individuals to act however they wanted. In the last systematic statement of his doctrine, *Commentary on the Work of Filangieri* (1822–4), a summary of his previous texts, Constant was categorical: the state's action should be reduced to the minimum, namely the maintenance of public order. 'Everything that goes beyond this limit is usurpation', 'everything else must be left free'.[8]

This demand thus concerns economic activities, too. It is not a matter of 'ensuring wealth', or of 'distributing it fairly', or even of 'preventing the excess of opulence'. The remedies for every lack will come from free individuals, so long as they are allowed to act without constraint. 'We can then trust individuals to find the good.' 'We must make no laws about industry.' All the country's economic problems will find their own solution. 'The remedy is competition.' Here lies Constant's second contribution to economic theory (in this respect he is much more radical than Adam Smith): economic prosperity is due solely to the action of individuals, and all state intervention must be prohibited. His book ends with this general conclusion: 'When it comes to thought, education and industry, the motto of governments must be: *Leave them be and leave them alone* (*laisser faire et laisser passer*).'[9] Such a logical conclusion presupposes not only that one believes in immutable laws directing human behaviour, but that human beings are moving in a single direction towards the 'progress of the human spirit', as Condorcet put it (even though he actually supported direct action on the part of the state). Nature is good and leads us to the good, unless an ignorant or malicious will prevents it – this is what the economic thinkers of the eighteenth century, from Mandeville to Smith, thought; they supported the theory of an 'invisible hand' which directed the unfolding of human affairs. Constant was here following the scientistic spirit that appeared in his period, a spirit that would be equally active in Marx.

Liberals presented their doctrine as a submission to the laws of nature; they thus resembled Augustinians, expecting everything from divine grace – with the difference that, as opposed to the pessimism of Augustine, they saw nature as benevolent and leading inevitably to progress. What they rejected were deliberate actions which risked disturbing nature's benevolent march. However, their arguments came up against a difficulty: the will itself is natural to men, and so the two categories, nature and will, are not opposed. The will to form plans is no less spontaneous than its absence. This is why a laissez-faire economy is no more 'natural' than a *dirigiste* economy. To have to *choose* between nature and will means that one has already chosen will; otherwise society would go in the desired direction all by itself. The real contrast is not between them, but between collective will (state will) and individual wills. Liberals who argue for a suspension of public intervention in the economic domain are not in favour of individual passivity – quite the opposite: those who pursue their objectives most energetically are the most worthy of praise. The state alone must submit itself to the laws of Providence, or the inflexible laws of history; as for individuals, they are required to show personal initiative. In this respect, the difference between neoliberals and socialists does not lie in the fact that the former are voluntarists and the latter are not; it lies in the fact that voluntarism, which they have in common, is mainly individual in one case and collective in the other. From this point of view, liberalism is a pseudo-naturalism and a real voluntarism.

Much more than in Constant, the almost religious character of belief in the victory of the good is evident in one radical defender of liberal thought from the following generation, the journalist Frédéric Bastiat, whose pithy formulations have attracted the attention of neoliberals today. Following the liberals preceding him, he thought, like Pelagius and unlike Augustine, that the world created by God was not evil; indeed, it is spontaneously evolving in the right direction. 'Whatever God does, is well done', he wrote in *The Law* of 1850.[10] 'Providence has not made any mistake, it has arranged things so that interests [. . .] are naturally combined in the most harmonious ways', he wrote in *Justice et fraternité* (*Justice and Fraternity*) in 1848. So his main idea is 'religious, for it assures us that it is not only the celestial but the social mechanism which reveals the wisdom of God, and declares His glory', as he added in *Economic Harmonies* (1850). In this way, Bastiat reveals the religious origin of formulas such as Adam Smith's 'invisible hand' or Marx's 'the meaning of history': they represent a secular version of the idea of a Providence leading human beings along the path established by God, even if they are unaware of it. The world advances inexorably towards the good, and we must not obstruct its march.

At the same time, just like Condorcet and Constant, who had replaced God with history, Bastiat aimed to found his conclusions on science. He wished to distinguish his own position from that of his socialist contemporaries, whom he accused of wasting time on fantasies and empty daydreams (they thought the complete opposite was the case). He came up with this paradoxical formula: 'I believe [. . .] with a scientific and reasonable belief' that 'evil leads to good and calls it forth', a formula reminiscent of the provocative subtitle of Mandeville's *Fable of the Bees*: 'private vices, public benefits'.

In 1848, the popular uprising in France led the National Assembly to ponder the advantages of introducing into the law, as well as the protection of civil liberties, the protection of social justice – thereby ensuring that the poor would have work or material help. Bastiat, elected as a deputy, opposed this measure vigorously. 'Human institutions must not go against divine laws', he wrote. If we start to organize charity, the drawbacks will be much more numerous than the advantages. If we favour mutual solidarity too much, we risk weakening the responsibility of each individual and killing off the spirit of enterprise. Pelagius recommended that we should not count too much on divine grace and should rely on personal effort. Bastiat fully agrees, except that in his work, social protection appears in place of divine mercy; for Bastiat, as for Pelagius, by creating man free and a world that is not really bad, God had finished his work. Bastiat was not concerned about future results: in society as he describes it, 'all careers would be open to everyone; each person could exercise his faculties freely [. . .]; there would be neither privileges, nor monopolies, nor restrictions of any kind' (*Justice et fraternité*).

Communism and neoliberalism

As I have mentioned, Communism became a reality in Russia in 1917. In its turn, this event galvanized liberal thinkers, who saw Communist practices as the embodiment of their worst fears: the total submission of individuals to the state, and at the same time the reduction of economics to the application of a plan decided in advance by a central organization. From this moment, a new phase in the evolution of liberalism began, which justifies the label *neoliberalism*. This doctrine was now formulated in opposition to the totalitarian world under construction: starting from various principles promoted by classical liberal thought, but radicalizing and hardening them, neoliberals developed their ideas within the context created by the October Revolution in Russia and the rise of Nazism in Germany. One of the works of Ludwig von Mises, their first great twentieth-century spokesman, is entitled *Socialism* (1922) and predicts the failure that threatens the state-controlled economy of Soviet Russia. Ayn Rand, another neoliberal propagandist, grew up in the Communist Russia that was responsible for the financial ruin of her family; while absorbing, during her studies, the predominant radical spirit of the time, she conceived a lasting hatred for it.[11]

Similarly, to take another emblematic example, the neoliberal manifesto by Friedrich A. Hayek, *The Road to Serfdom*, published during the war (1944), presents itself primarily as a warning against anything that might resemble totalitarian practices: first the Nazi enemy, but also – for Hayek the relationship between the two was obvious – the socialist ally, namely the Soviet Union. Hayek condemns the tendency shared by these regimes to divide humanity into friends and enemies, a tendency that allows them to implement the logic of war in domestic policy; he criticizes the reduction of truth, justice and morality to purely historical configurations placed at the service of the political goals of the moment; and he deplores the suppression of individual freedoms. He also notes the contrast between the two interpretations of the meaning of history: class struggle culminating in confrontation in the one case, a harmonious convergence of interests in the other.

The target of his fiercest attacks is the economic doctrine adopted by these regimes, which according to him are different variations of 'socialism'. The main features of the doctrine are defined as follows: the socialists demand that private property should be abolished, or severely restricted; that the state should become the sole or at least the main employer in the country; and that free enterprise, competition and the market economy should be replaced by what Hayek calls 'planning', a fully state-controlled economy, unified and hierarchical, led by a few individuals who decide in advance on the directions that the country will pursue. Depriving its citizens of all economic autonomy, the totalitarian state condemns them to political slavery. Hayek thus seeks to show why such an economic choice would inevitably lead to disaster, even in a democracy.

This critique of totalitarianism is fair and necessary. However, looking at the various elements of neoliberal doctrine, one is led to wonder if the opposition between these two models of government is always as complete as those who formulate it believe. 'Each in its own way, the Communist ideology and the doctrine that opposes it depend on the Promethean myth', writes Flahault in his study of this myth;[12] they are heirs also, one might add, to the legacy of Pelagius.

Several commentators have already emphasized the odd conception of history that underlies neoliberal doctrines. As we have seen in connection with Bastiat, these doctrines postulate that if only men did not interfere, obstructing the natural course of things with their projects and plans, all would be for the best in the best of all possible worlds. This natural course consists in the absence of any obstacle placed in the way of free competition, or any state intervention to correct adverse effects. 'It is the submission of man to impersonal market forces which in the past has made possible the development of a civilization', writes Hayek.[13] It seems that, like God, the market can do no wrong. From this point of view, neoliberalism, which presents its objectives as entirely 'natural', is not really opposed to the Communist theory, whose 'theoretical conclusions', as we have seen, are deemed to express, 'in general terms, actual relations springing from an existing class struggle'. And since man obeys the laws of nature, it is enough to be apprised of these to know what direction to go in. After the 'scientific socialism' of Marx and Engels, we then have 'scientific' liberalism: the two share the same premises.

Yet we have seen that this claim of a total submission to the forces of nature does not really fit neoliberal ideology as a whole: this abdication of voluntary actions concerns only collective agents; as for individuals, far from recommending they adopt a docile obedience to fate, neoliberals sing the praises of their freedom and spirit of initiative. They thus add yet another twist to their programme of submission to nature, which again brings them closer to the socialists. Marxist doctrine combines belief in an inescapable sense of history, which it is essential to know so as to submit to it, with a demand for a voluntarist intervention that can speed up history. For their part, neoliberals distance themselves from the laissez-faire of classical liberalism and advocate a form of state intervention, namely the systematic elimination of any barrier to competition. 'The attitude of a liberal towards society', Hayek writes – spinning a metaphor that would not have been disdained by Soviet leaders – 'is like that of the gardener who tends a plant and in order to create the conditions most favourable to its growth must know as much as possible about its structure and functions'; his objective, it is true, is different: 'deliberately creating a system within which competition will work as beneficially as possible'.[14] This combination of blind faith in the laws of nature and history, and the belief that we can achieve all the goals that we set ourselves, is a characteristic of scientism, common to Communists and neoliberals: since science can know everything, technology can achieve everything. The remodelling of society is just one technical problem among others.

In itself, such a decision is not really surprising: as Hayek admits, 'everybody who is not a complete fatalist is a planner, every political act is (or ought to be) an act of planning'.[15] The reforms imposed in the late twentieth century by political leaders such as Thatcher, Reagan and Pinochet in their respective states are evidence of this voluntarist attitude. The same goes for the famous 'shock therapy' applied in the countries of Eastern Europe after the fall of the Wall, or the actions taken by Western states in 2008–9 to deal with the financial crisis and rescue the private banks. Now, while profits remain individual, risks are socialized. This is a 'state neoliberalism', a contradiction in terms that casts doubt on the internal consistency of the project. Constant had not foreseen that the state could simultaneously strengthen its grip on the lives of individuals *and* place itself in the service of some of them. In the aftermath of 11 September 2001, the states that have adopted this ideology, such as the United States and Britain, have increased their control over civil liberties, while continuing to grant full freedom to individual economic agents. From this time, we entered *ultraliberalism*, the third phase in the evolution of this doctrine.

Neoliberalism also shares with Marxism the belief that the social existence of men depends mainly on the economy. It is not just a matter of isolating the economy from other human activities, but of assigning a dominant role to it. This domination appears in Marxist doctrine, even if the practice of Communist states did not really exemplify it. The principle is found among the theorists of neoliberalism, and this time it is put into practice. It is no coincidence that the major work by the founder of this school of thought, Ludwig von Mises, has the title *Human Action* and the subtitle 'A Treatise on Economics' (1949). For his part, Hayek is ready to criticize the excessive emphasis on economic needs and structures in 'planning', writing: 'The ultimate ends of the activities of reasonable beings are never economic'; yet it is significant that the only other goal he identifies is the desire for 'general opportunity' and 'power'.[16] And most importantly, he forgets even this minimal addendum when he turns to the effects of the pure market economy: 'the only ties which hold the whole of a Great Society together are purely "economic"', he writes.[17]

The fundamentalist temptation

There is one more feature of neoliberalism reminiscent of totalitarian discourse, namely its radicalism, and the Manichaeism that accompanies it. In fact, human beings have both social and economic needs, both individual and collective lives: the two viewpoints limit and complement one another mutually. But this overlap is ignored by theorists on both sides. Collectivism alone is good in the eyes of some, individualism alone for others. Under the Communist regime, individual existence was entirely under the control of the community; in the stock neoliberal worldview, any collective influence on individual desires is immediately seen as bringing with it the threat of the gulag. Communist society suppressed individual liberties; but to tell individuals 'anything goes' does not ensure that they will flourish.

The autonomy of economic action was challenged by the Communist regime, which favoured political choices (the result was permanent shortages). In ultraliberalism, it is political autonomy that is shaken, under pressure from several sides. Today, globalization, another feature of this new period, means that the actors of economic life easily evade the control of local governments: at the first hiccup, the multinational company moves its factories to a more welcoming country. It is entrepreneurs who nowadays implement the old Marxist slogan, by imposing the unification of all the workers of the world . . .

Thus the now global economy is no longer subject to the political control of states; on the contrary, it is the states who have placed themselves at its service. These states are dependent on unrated agencies that guide their choices, while not themselves being subject to any political control. They are now democracies only in name – it is no longer the people who hold power. They can, if needs be, defend their borders – but money does not stop there. With this unified market, an individual or group of individuals who do not have the least political legitimacy are able, with a single click on their computers, to transfer their capital elsewhere or keep it at home, and thereby choose whether or not to plunge a country into unemployment and recession. They can cause social unrest or help to forestall it. They are individuals equipped with immense power who are accountable to no one.

Within each country, ultraliberal ideology does not leave much room for political action either. The universal motto here is: outside the market, there is no salvation. Turning their backs on checks and balances that were obvious to Adam Smith and his contemporaries, they seek to root out any intervention by the state that might 'distort free competition'; they even see it as the cause of the financial crisis unleashed in 2007. In so doing, they overlook the recent changes in the economy and forget that all 'products' are not of the same nature. The very logic of consumption – 'always more!' – is never called into question. According to this new creed, the state should intervene only to promote the free operation of competition, to oil the wheels of a natural clock (the market), and to alleviate social conflicts and maintain public order: its role is not to limit, but to facilitate economic power.

Just like other men, the political leaders of democratic countries are not immune to the attraction of money; but today, reassured by ultraliberal ideology, they are even more happy to serve the powers of money, as evidenced by various well-known incidents in France (several tax reforms, the Woerth-Bettencourt affair, etc.). The result this time is, on the one hand, the establishment of political and economic oligarchies and, on the other, the marginalization of losers, those real waste products of the system, condemned to both poverty and scorn: they are the cause of their own misfortune and, to help them, we should appeal neither to the state nor to collective solidarity. The cult of the superman suits the logic of the ultraliberals.

This change is, in a sense, even more fundamental than that imposed by the French Revolution. The Revolution was happy just to replace the sovereignty of the monarch with that of the people: but ultraliberalism places the sovereignty of economic forces, embodied in the will of individuals, above political sovereignty, whatever its nature. In doing so, it – paradoxically – violates the basic principle of liberal thought, which is the limitation of one power by another. Classical liberalism is founded on the heterogeneity of society: common interests do not always coincide with particular interests, and liberalism seeks to limit the action of the general will by the defence of individual liberties, and vice versa. Its new avatar wants to prevent the general will from limiting the actions of individuals; as it does not recognize the existence of a common interest, it reduces society to the sum of the people composing it. The very foundations of democracy are thereby undermined. We rightly condemn political regimes where all social life is subject to ideological tutelage, whether religious, as in theocracies, or doctrinal, as in totalitarianism. But we seem to see no problem in a situation where the principle of the unlimited market imposes its exclusive sway. As the American commentator Benjamin Barber puts it, 'when it comes to markets dominating everything, from ubiquitous advertising and a consumption always provided with its very own secular sharia law, we call this freedom'.[18]

Faced with the disproportionate economic power held by individuals or groups of individuals with immense capital at their disposal, political power often turns out to be too weak. In the United States, in the name of the unlimited freedom of expression, the Supreme Court allowed the corporate funding of candidates for election; concretely, this means that those who have more money can impose the candidates of their choice. The president of the country, certainly one of the most powerful men in the world, had to abandon his attempts to promote a fair reform of the medical insurance system, to regulate the activity of banks, and to reduce the environmental damage caused by the lifestyle of the country's citizens. But the patient who cannot afford healthcare is not free, nor is the man thrown out onto the streets because he is unable to repay his bank loan. This leads to the paradox where individual freedom, in the name of which all state intervention is rejected, is hampered by the unrestricted freedom granted to the market and businesses.

Ultraliberalism justifies its demand for unlimited freedom to launch a business, to trade and to manage its capital not by defending the right to selfishness, but by saying that this freedom is the most effective way to enrich society as a whole. It opposes any measure of regulation by the government because, according to its supporters, this will impoverish the entire population. Does experience confirm this theory? Flahault invites us to consider two examples. The first is that of the slave trade between the sixteenth and nineteenth centuries. It corresponded perfectly to the requirements of economic efficiency.

> European traders brought Africans goods in exchange for which the latter delivered other goods to them. European ships carried them across the Atlantic, where they were sold at a profit. These goods were then used to produce sugar to be sold in Europe, where demand was high. With this international division of labour, the result of the free play of supply and demand, everyone gained – African merchants, producers in the Caribbean and America, financiers, ship owners and European consumers.[19]

However, given this example, one would hesitate to say, as Milton Friedman, a recent disciple of Bastiat, said of the ultraliberal system, that it 'brings harmony and peace to the world'. If the Atlantic traffic was eventually halted, this was not as a result of the freedom enjoyed by those involved in it, but thanks to the intervention, on moral and political grounds, of other actors in social life, and ultimately of the states themselves, and thus the general will. The prohibition of trafficking ensured the freedom of the slaves, and the absence of binding legislation ensured the freedom of traders, who were, in addition, much more powerful than the slaves.

The second example concerns ecology. It is unlikely that, without state intervention, market agents would allow the need to protect the environment to trump their immediate interests – especially since it is often the environment of a distant country or in an uncertain future that is at stake. We have many examples to the contrary, including the present state of the entrepreneur's own country. Not only does he do nothing of his own free will to protect this environment, but he often uses his power and some of his gains to remove any barriers to his action. For example, in 2006, in the oil province of Alberta, Canada, a doctor was alarmed to see cancer rates increase by 30 per cent. 'Too bad for him. Health Canada, the federal government, is prosecuting him for an "unprofessional attitude" causing "undue concern."'[20] One might well ask whether the oil company did not intervene beforehand . . .

In April 2010 a BP platform exploded in the Gulf of Mexico, causing the largest oil spill in the history of the United States; it was discovered that the governmental commission that issues permissions for drilling and controls the oil companies is essentially composed of former employees of these very same companies. Unlimited freedom of economic agents does not guarantee – to put it mildly – the protection of the environment, even though this is a common good. Left unchecked, oil companies go for inexpensive and thus unreliable building materials. No wonder: businesses are not individuals with a conscience, and feel no remorse about being guided solely by the profit motive. The limitation of this appetite can come only from a body not in thrall to economic logic.

The secret relationship between Communism and neoliberalism can help us better understand the impressive ease with which, after the fall of the Wall, the new ideology began to replace the old in the countries of Eastern Europe. The collective interest was there viewed with suspicion: to hide its depravity, the previous regime had invoked collective interest so often that no one took it seriously, and saw only a hypocritical mask. If the only thing driving behaviour is, in any case, the search for profit and the thirst for power, if the ruthless struggle for the survival of the fittest is the true (and harsh) law of existence, we may as well stop pretending and openly endorse the 'law of the jungle'. The former Communist apparatchiks were thus able to deck themselves out quickly in the clothes of ultraliberalism.

By requiring blind adherence to its assumptions, presented as scientific truths, not as the voluntary choices of certain values at the expense of others, ultraliberalism in its turn becomes a secular religion, sometimes spread through promotion strategies reminiscent of those used by the Communists. The presence of these common features is not enough, of course, to call ultraliberalism a form of totalitarianism, even of the 'soft' variety. But it suggests that the two are not as radically opposed as the adherents of each doctrine claim. Ultraliberalism is not just an enemy of totalitarianism; it is also, at least in some aspects, its brother: a mirror image, opposite and equal. Its project takes us from one extreme to the other, from the totalitarian 'all for the state' to the ultraliberal 'all for the individual', from a 'liberticidal' regime to another one that we might call 'sociocidal'.

Neoliberalism's blind spots

Neoliberals have inherited another characteristic of revolutionary thinkers: like the latter, they call on abstract values which are assumed to hold a universal attraction, namely, freedom. It was by examining the revolutionary inclination to appeal to general values that Edmund Burke, at the time of the French Revolution (in 1790), formulated his reservations about freedom. He accepts it as a value too, but he writes, 'But I cannot stand forward and give praise or blame to anything which relates to human actions, and human concerns, on a simple view of the object, as it stands stripped of every relation, in all the nakedness and solitude of metaphysical abstraction.' Politics is not so much a matter of principles as of their application. In a particular society, freedom is not the only value worth defending; it interacts with various forces and competes with other demands. In addition, and this is essential, 'liberty, when men act in bodies, is power. Considerate people, before they declare themselves, will observe the use which is made of power.'[21] In its turn, power must be judged by how it is used, not in the abstract. Neither Constant nor Bastiat ever considers the other side of freedom: if nothing limits my action, I gain an ever-increasing power that is exercised, whether I like it or not, to the detriment of other people around me. These thinkers thereby forget the golden rule formulated by Montesquieu for governments that aim to be moderate: 'all unlimited power must be unlawful'.[22]

When Bastiat said that, in his country, anyone could pursue any career and anyone could always exercise his faculties freely, he was imagining abstract men, deprived of origin, family background or social relationships, men as they have never existed. It is not only the socialists of his time who opposed this 'metaphysical abstraction' and suggested abandoning this unquestioned assumption in order to help the poor; Christian activists did so too, sensitive as they were to the economic distress of their contemporaries. The Dominican priest Henri Dominique Lacordaire published at this time his *Conferences of Notre Dame*, which were a great success. In the fifty-second conference, from 1848, he confronts the question of formal freedoms and real freedoms in these terms:

> Ask the worker whether he is free to leave work at the dawn of the day which enjoins him to rest. [. . .] Ask those decrepit beings who inhabit the industrial cities whether they are free to save their souls by relieving their bodies. Ask the countless victims of personal greed and the greed of a master whether they are free to become better.

And he concludes with this formula that has since become famous: 'Between the strong and the weak, between the rich and the poor, between the master and the servant, it is freedom which oppresses and the law that liberates.'[23] The freedom which the rich and strong demand for themselves is a way of increasing their power within society. We must therefore, as Augustine also wished, set a limit to the human will, though Lacordaire, despite being a priest, finds this limit not in God but in social justice and human laws. Here we see Burke's wish granted: the demand for freedom must be put into context.

Another erroneous abstraction lies in imagining human beings as selfish individuals motivated only by their material interests (at that time called 'rational'). But can well-being derive solely from the satisfaction of one's desires for material goods and power? It is as if the proponents of neoliberalism had slipped unconsciously from the idea that 'competition is beneficial to the economy' to the principle that 'what is good for the economy is all that is needed for the happiness of human beings'. In doing so, they neglect a huge part of human existence, one that is only schematically summed up in the phrase 'social life'. But it is obviously impossible to postulate an asocial 'human nature', or an individual who (like one of the lower animals) is reduced to his own basic needs.

At the basis of neoliberal thought there is indeed a problematic anthropology, which presents man as a self-sufficient being, essentially alone, with only an occasional need for other beings around him. This contradicts everything that psychology, sociology and history, not to mention common sense, teach us about human identity, and of which the classical liberals, Locke and Montesquieu, Adam Smith and Benjamin Constant, were well aware. They knew that the human being is an inter-human being. Humanism, which is the great European intellectual tradition, contrasts at this specific point with individualism, insisting as it does on the fully social nature of human being: the relationship between them is prior to the construction of the self, a human being cannot emerge without the recognition that he finds in the eyes of others around him. So he imposes on the autonomy of each person restrictions that stem from our inevitably shared lives: the individual is not only the source of action, he must also be its goal; the demand for universality in turn limits the exercise of freedom. The principles of equality and fraternity are not less fundamental to democracy than is the principle of liberty; if we forget them, the aspiration to ensure that all can enjoy freedom is itself condemned to failure.

Not all human desires stem from economic needs, nor can society be reduced to a mere collection of individuals, each self-sufficient. Hayek dismisses as meaningless abstractions such expressions as 'common good', 'general interest' or 'social justice' – but what could be more abstract than the individuals he mentions, without any historical dimension or any social belonging? Human beings do not exist in isolation, they are made up of past encounters and exchanges, they have inherited and borrowed many things, they interact with and are dependent on their fellows in the present. Society as imagined by the neoliberals is like a club of voluntary members who may also decide to suspend their membership, as they are self-sufficient. The reference to any social and cultural belonging is suppressed, the need for recognition from those among whom we live is ignored, the search for the common good is abandoned – lest they lead to totalitarianism. Unlimited paeans to individual freedom end up creating a purely imaginary being, as if the ultimate goal of life were to free oneself, like Robinson Crusoe on his desert isle, from any link and any dependency rather than being caught up in the dense network of social relationships, friendships and loves.[24] By refusing to set up any barriers to individual action, neoliberals commit themselves unhesitatingly to the path once traced by Pelagius.

Contrary to the image of man that we find at the basis of neoliberal doctrine, he is not the product of his own will, but always and only constitutes himself within the family environment and social context in which he is born. The clearest example of this reality is language, which predates the individual; if he were not immersed, from his first wails onwards, in an environment of words, he would be sentenced to an almost animal condition. Before acting on the social fabric in which we live, each of us has been shaped by it. Of course, the action of this fabric is not limited to language: there is also the set of rules and norms that allow us to consti-tute ourselves as group members. 'The law makes each of us a legal subject', writes one legal scholar, Alain Supiot. 'To be free, the subject must first be bound by words that attach him to other men.'[25] Lacordaire was right in giving priority to law over liberty: forgetting the law leaves the field open to arbitrary power.

Freedom and attachment

A long-standing debate had contrasted two conceptions of the place of the attachment that humans feel for each other. According to Christian doctrine, as interpreted by Pascal, 'Therefore all that incites us to attach ourselves to the creatures is bad; since it prevents us from serv-ing God if we know Him, or from seeking Him if we know Him not.' Pascal himself, according to his sister, could be tender and loving to his family, but he fled attachment, whether he was the subject or the object of it, and even gently reproached his sister, less perfect than he was, because she gave way to human, all-too-human feelings for her brother. 'It is unjust that men should attach themselves to me, even though they do it with pleasure and voluntarily. I should deceive those in whom I had created this desire; for I am not the end of any, and I have not the wherewithal to satisfy them.'[26]

According to the humanist doctrine embodied in Rousseau, man is a legitimate goal for man and, far from being an unfortunate attitude, attachment is inherent in the human condition. True, Rousseau wrote that 'every affection is a sign of insufficiency; if each of us had no need of others, we should hardly think of associating with them'. But that is the way we are: born inadequate, dying inadequate, always driven by the needs of others, in pursuit of what we need to make us whole. It is because they come into existence with a congenital deficiency that human beings need others, need to be considered, and also need to attach their hearts to others.[27] And any link restricts freedom.

The development of attachment in a world that no longer has a special relationship with God does not mean you need to accept passively, and even glorify, all the links imposed on the individual from childhood, to see solidarity with family, clan, ethnicity or race as compulsory. The most valuable relations, as Montaigne said, are those that depend on 'our own choice and voluntary freedom'.[28] But how has anyone ever imagined that the ideal of a fulfilled life is total 'independence', that is to say the absence of any obligation and any attachment, not only to God but to fellow human beings? This is why unlimited freedom cannot be an ideal for human existence – any more than it is the starting point.

In a political essay, Benjamin Constant said: 'Individual independence is the first of modern needs.' In his novel, *Adolphe*, the main character noted: 'How my heart cried out for that dependence which I had often hated! [. . .] I was free indeed, I was no longer loved: I was a stranger to the whole world.'[29] This contradiction, or at least this tension, runs through all Constant's work: while his

political and critical writings ardently defend the idea of
the autonomous individual, his anthropology, as found
in his fiction, his personal writings and his great work
on religion, has a different idea of the human being. He
is born within society, which therefore precedes him:
'The development of intelligence is itself the result of
society', and his identity is inherently relational: man
always has 'a need for attachment in his heart', and
'everything depends on reciprocity in life'.[30] And if we
were to seek an ideal towards which private life tends,
it would be love more than freedom. As Constant wrote
in a letter to a woman friend: 'A word, a look, a hand-
shake have in my view always seemed preferable to all
reason and all the thrones on earth.'[31]

5

The Effects of Neoliberalism

Blame it on science?

I would now like to look more quickly at some worrying aspects of contemporary life in democracies. Without being a direct result of neoliberal ideology, these aspects take on a new importance in the framework imposed by this doctrine. The facts themselves are known: it is their overall significance that will preoccupy us here.

An unexpected illustration of the dangers created by neoliberalism was the accident at the nuclear power plant in Fukushima, Japan, in March 2011. At first glance, this catastrophe, like others that preceded it, was an example of the risks involved in the Pelagian attitude adopted by a large part of humanity since the Enlightenment: it is all too tempting to rely on the discoveries of science in the material world and ask it to facilitate the fulfilment of all our desires. The progress of the scientific spirit, put into practice by industrial society, was expected to bring prosperity and comfort to all. This aspiration was thus an example of hubris or excess, and was akin to the political messianism that, at the same time, wanted to bring to distant peoples the supposed benefits of European civilization. However, after the euphoria of the nineteenth century, it was necessary to face facts: technological progress does not uniformly create benefits, and may sometimes even lead to new threats.

Control of atomic fission is the clearest example of this dangerous and menacing excess. Physicists who, in the period between the two world wars, had helped unlock the secrets of the material world were faced with a big moral dilemma when, in 1945, the effects of their discovery allowed the action of a single atomic bomb to destroy in a matter of seconds hundreds of thousands of lives. Given such an outcome, could anyone rejoice at the progress of science, or believe it always contributes to the progress of humanity? The situation is exacerbated when disasters are the effect, not of an explosion caused intentionally, but of a peaceful endeavour meant to serve the common good, as in nuclear power plants. The accidents at Three Mile Island in 1979, Chernobyl in 1986 and Fukushima in 2011 showed that the peaceful use of the atom involves risks that it is impossible to predict or control.

The immediate results of the last accident are well known: hundreds of square kilometres of the overpopulated country of Japan became uninhabitable, and the sea and its wildlife were contaminated, not to mention the people who worked or lived there. Indeed, if the winds had blown the wrong way or if the ocean currents had flowed in a different direction, the results would have been much worse. The indirect consequences of the disaster are incalculable, ranging from a change in eating habits in Japan (natural foods, fish and plants, have become the primary sources of risk) to the disruption of energy policy in other countries, such as Germany, which has decided to close its nuclear plants. This does not end the debate, since nuclear plants must be replaced by other energy sources which may be more polluting and may just worsen the planet's climate a little more.

The use of nuclear energy is obviously not the first

example of a technical improvement which brings previously unknown risks in its wake. After all, when men boarded a ship to cross the sea, they risked being drowned. The same goes for all those who, today, have no hesitation about flying: technology cannot be entirely trusted, planes crash, and the chances of survival are then usually nil. But until now, people risked only their own lives. What is serious about nuclear power plants (or nuclear bombs) is that they trigger a process that cannot be stopped: the radioactivity released will last twenty-four thousand years, or in practical terms forever. The risks I take today will concern eight hundred generations of my descendants. They also concern, as we saw with Chernobyl, the residents of countries other than those that have chosen to use nuclear energy.

Another source of energy that we hear more and more about has the similar drawback that something negative results from a very deliberate choice: shale gas, which is buried deep in the ground and can be brought to the surface by controlled underground explosions. Where this operation has begun, residents have complained that their tap water has become undrinkable as the water tables are contaminated. Since the waste is stored above ground, air and earth in turn may become a source of danger. These elements whose presence seemed assured forever, water, air and earth, appear vulnerable, so great is the power now available to human beings. Not to mention the indirect effects, such as falling prices for houses in the contaminated areas, houses in which a lifetime's whole savings have been invested, or indeed the savings of several generations.

There are countless areas in which innovations are both a promise and a threat. By modifying the actual structure of plants, and not, as since the Neolithic period, just their environment or their selection, we get GMOs, genetically modified organisms that improve crops and get rid of pests. But by so radically disturbing the balance of species, the result of adaptations that have taken thousands of years, we may cause new disasters. Prospects both enticing and frightening are opening up through the genetic manipulation of the human embryo, so that it will one day be possible to choose the sex of the child or the desired degree of its intelligence. Nanotechnology will facilitate the production of bionic men and women with unprecedented performance levels. Are we sure this is a good thing? Instruments that are external to the human body still act on it: mobile phones could, it seems, cause brain tumours, and prolonged interaction with computers certainly affects the social behaviour of their users . . .

All of these changes have aroused strong reactions. One could say that the growing importance of environmental issues in the public debate is directly related to them. The figure of the sorcerer's apprentice who unleashes uncontrollable forces has been given renewed prominence, as has Frankenstein, the scientist whose creature escapes from its creator, or – in fiction movies – robots who rise up in rebellion against their masters. The German sociologist Ulrich Beck suggested in the 1980s that Western societies had left behind the period of 'first modernity', when science and technology were expected to contribute to prosperity and progress, and had entered a 'second modernity' or a 'risk society', where these activities are seen as sources of danger. Men's tools become their worst enemies. Previously, the problem stemmed from nature; human willpower, supported by science, was a source of salvation. Today, it is the opposite: science is perceived as a risk, and it is nature that brings hope. Should we conclude that we have come full circle, and that Pelagius must again give way to Augustine (though now it is nature, rather than grace, that has replaced the will)?

Yet we cannot lay the blame for disasters like Fukushima, or other abuses of technology, on the human will in general as it seeks to meet human needs, or on the progress of science. More specific actions have played a decisive role here. The accident occurred at Fukushima following an earthquake and the tsunami that accompanied it. However, this plant was constructed on a particular site – next to the sea, in a place prone to tremors, not far from major cities – for reasons of convenience and, ultimately, because this was the most cost-effective solution for those running it. The explosion was not the effect of a natural disaster (nature does not recognize the concept of disaster), but of a series of human decisions. In the final analysis, it resulted from a collusion between private operators and government bureaucrats. The extraction of shale gas is a source of wealth for those who practise it; they prefer to bribe politicians and compensate the local residents rather than thinking about the long-term effects of their actions. The same goes for other technological abuses: it is not the zeal for knowledge, but the desire to get rich, that motivates the immediate and immoderate use of new technologies, without any concern for their impact on other human beings, present or future. And it is not only greed that makes people act this way: those responsible for such choices are also blinded by the vertigo of power, the pride they draw from being in control of such mighty forces and deciding the future of a large population.

To fight against the harmful effects of these practices, scientific knowledge is indispensable. It needs to indicate the possible consequences, and the causes, of global warming. It needs also to discover the effects, desirable or undesirable, of GMOs. We cannot replace science with nature, but we can replace bad science with another, better science: the former does not care about the impact of its discoveries beyond the here and now, the latter takes into consideration the length of time and the extent of space, generations yet to come, and our neighbours. The Fukushima disaster and others like it are not due to human aspirations for a better life, or to the quest to discover the secrets of matter, but to the neoliberal logic that looks at humanity as an undifferentiated mass of individuals themselves reduced to their own economic interests.

It is not the task of nature, but of the common will to protect us against the excesses of individual wills. Just as the totalitarian nightmare does not compromise the value of collective action, the bomb at Hiroshima and the explosion at Fukushima do not undermine the acquisition of knowledge, but require that we seek to expand its scope. This can also be understood in a literal sense: human technological power is such that its effects do not stop at the border of a small country but act on a continental scale. An accident in a nuclear power plant in France directly concerns the German population, just as global warming caused by German industry has consequences for the people of France. The Chernobyl cloud crossed all the European borders without hindrance. The collective will to guide decisions for tomorrow's world must also think on a continental scale.

The law retreats

To forget the constitutive social dimension of every human being is not only to commit an intellectual error. There is a real danger that, on the basis of this mutilated image of what founds our humanity, we will embark on a policy whose effects will also be mutilating. Let us look at a few examples.

The Western tradition distinguishes between two main types of social relationships that produce relations of obligation, depending on whether they are governed by a *law* or by a *contract*. In all cases, we can identify three participants: an *I* and a *you* to begin with, two partners who interact – the seller and the buyer, the master and the slave, the teacher and the student; then a *he*, *she* or *they*, the impersonal third party, which guarantees the validity of the commitments. But this third party does not play the same role in both cases. As Supiot notes, by law we mean 'texts and words that are imposed on us independent of our control', while a contract refers to 'those who make a voluntary agreement with others'.[1] In the case of the law, the third party fixes the contents of the obligation: what is forbidden, or allowed, or imposed, along with the need to comply. In the case of a contract, the contracting parties freely decide on the contents, while the third party is limited to endorsing the validity of the contracts: if you do not keep your word, you are dealt with under the law. The law reflects the will of the people, a contract is based on the freedom of individuals.

This distinction reflects the fact that certain norms and values are not subject to negotiation between individuals, as they have been previously decided, even before these individuals came into the world, and regardless of their will. Which in turn reminds us that society cannot be reduced to the sum of the individuals who belong to it, contrary to what is suggested by the oft-quoted phrase of the former British prime minister, the ultraliberal Margaret Thatcher: 'There is no such thing as society.' For this reason, we have not only rights stemming from our shared humanity – what we call human rights – but also (and especially) the rights and obligations arising from our membership of a particular society.

In pre-modern societies, the role of guarantor of all obligations is played by traditions and sometimes by one or more gods. In many human societies, a major change has occurred: this role is now entrusted to society itself (or the 'people'), which has the sovereign power to choose the order that will govern it; in practice, this role is vested in the state. The trust we place in the state (for example, the fixed value of the currency, or

even the possibility of appealing to the law) is no more
rational than the belief in God; it is imposed on us by
necessity: for society to function, everyone must believe
that someone guarantees the rules by which we live. If
the third party guarantor were to disappear, we would
be reduced to the animal kingdom, what we improperly
call the 'law of the jungle', a state in which force alone
counts. The totalitarian regime approaches this state
most closely: the head of state is bound neither by the
laws nor by his own promises; his will alone counts, as
manifested in the present moment. If we define barbarism as the refusal to consider that others are human
beings like us, we can see this world governed by power
alone as a near-perfect embodiment of barbarism.

Every society knows these two types of relations, governed either by impersonal law or by contract between
individuals, but they are not found everywhere in the
same proportions. In traditional societies, the field of
law is much more restricted. The size of the group is
limited, everyone knows everyone else, people negotiate
together to find a solution to conflict. There is 'blood
money': in the case of murder, you do not complain to
the justice system, but you are compensated with two
cows or ten sheep. Such negotiation is obviously impossible in those complex and extensive societies that are
the great modern states: just as a common, impersonal
currency replaces barter between neighbours, abstract
law plays the role assumed by agreements between residents of the same village.

This contrast between societies has not disappeared
from the modern world. In my teenage years in Bulgaria,
I felt a constant irritation at the uncertainty surround-
ing the application of the law. Partly out of an 'oriental'
tradition, partly to escape the rigours of the totalitarian
state, Bulgarians seemed tempted by perpetual negotiation: you never knew what to expect. The surly
official could smile on you if you slipped him a bribe.

Administrative obstacles could be overcome if you had a relative, or a friend of a friend, who could say a word to the appropriate person. All this was tiring and frustrating. Great was my relief when I came to live in France, where life was lived according to fixed rules, known to all! True, the downside was that human relationships were colder and more distant, but I got used to that. After a few years, I discovered, however, that the contrast was less clear than I had thought. On the – highly symbolic – occasion of my application for naturalization, I received a visit from two strangers (though they were French citizens!) who told me that they worked at police headquarters: they offered, in return for money, to speed things up for me . . . So Bulgarian habits were not unknown in France! Except that these practices (which I would like to believe marginal) were practised in a society dominated by law, and neither brought people together nor introduced any more human warmth into their relations – quite the contrary.

At quite another level, the past few decades have, in Western democracies, witnessed a change that consists in expanding the extent of contracts and reducing the extent of laws, which means at the same time restricting the power of the people and giving free rein to the will of individuals. This development occurs particularly in the workplace, where employers often complain about the plethora of regulations that impede their freedom of action; they would rather negotiate a contract directly with their employees. The practice also extends to justice: when you have caused injury to someone, it becomes possible to escape conviction if you choose to repair the damage and compensate the injured party. It is true that in this way we manage to unclog the overworked law courts. But a crime is not only a wrong done to someone, it is also an infringement of the rule of common life, a tear in the social fabric, and *this* damage is not repaired by compensation. Whoever is able to pay escapes any punishment: he simply has to pay the piper. Only the poor go to jail.

This development has received a major boost with the globalization of the economy. Ideally, the economy is not under any state or legislation, so it uses only contracts. Regardless of the country, it deals always and only with individuals, all alike, all driven by the same material interests. The disproportion between the powers of the parties involved, however, is glaring: the powerful multinational corporation and the unemployed job seeker do not really come into the same category. In the place of God as guarantor, we now find not the state, but the market, that is to say, the mode of exchange itself, which becomes its own foundation. Lacordaire's remarks are fully relevant here.

Loss of meaning

Similar trends can be observed in the workplace. Acts carried out to produce goods or procure services bring a return to those who perform them. This includes, of course, remuneration, but also a contribution – not given any formal shape, but no less important – to their psychological and social equilibrium. Even those who work alone, craftsmen or artists, enjoy the awareness that they are making themselves useful; even those who, in their profession, do not address people directly, can if they perform their task find gratification in a job well done: a straight wall, a door that closes properly, a car that restarts. This sentiment is strengthened when, as in the vast majority of cases, we participate in a collective effort, in a business or administration. The individual is part of a community, and the recognition given to him by his colleagues intensifies his sense of existing. These moments spent together are not simply enjoyable (when they actually are so), they are necessary for the construction of identity. A business does not produce them mechanically (we cannot be cheerful to order), but it can provide the objective conditions in which the person can flourish and be enriched.

The anthropology underlying neoliberal doctrine, in which the economy dominates social life and material cost-effectiveness dominates the economy, has a strong influence on the world of work. This concerns both the place *of* work among other human activities and the place *in* work of the symbolic benefits which we have just mentioned. The new requirement to impose greater 'flexibility' and 'mobility' on the personnel of a business is a good example of the dramatic changes experienced by work itself. To produce greater productivity, to ensure that routines and stereotypes do not become encrusted, a business will often shift its workers from one position to another (flexibility) or change their workplace (mobility). We think this will help them work better; they themselves may also be tempted by higher salaries. In addition, these concepts have become a mark of modernity and efficiency, as opposed to ambient traditionalism or conservatism; so people accept them without questioning their overall cost. Thus, in France Telecom, hundreds of executives change jobs every six months. As a result, the need for flexibility leads to people forgetting the need for a competence that has been acquired over a long period of practice.

One effect of flexibility is that the social network constructed day by day is weakened, and with it the very identity of the individual. We forget that a job is not just an abstract task, but also a living environment made of human relations, common rites, obligations and prohibitions. The effects of mobility, which are also often hard on family life, are even more devastating. Thus, in France Telecom, there were twenty-five suicides in twenty months, not to mention cases of depression and other health problems. We can see how simplistic and disconcerting is the slogan 'work more to earn more', launched by the French president Sarkozy: earning more is good, but if it comes at the price of a ruined family life, a loss of meaning at work and a lack of recognition, it is doubtful whether it is worth it.

The same can be said of the requirement to prioritize work over all one's other activities. 'Good' employees, the ones who will get promotion, are the ones who are ready to sacrifice their evenings to attend urgent meetings, and spend their weekends at home preparing for the coming week. Their family life inevitably suffers. Both parents, but especially fathers, when they are in positions of responsibility, no longer see their children except for Sunday mornings. This poses a problem for the professional careers of women, who are less inclined to sacrifice their family life. Yet some feminists encourage them to do so. A German woman journalist who had held senior posts wondered why so few businesses in her country have women on their executive committees, and sorrowfully noted: 'Even those who are educated and supposedly emancipated choose, for the sake of comfort, to follow the model of the wife at home, looking after the children.'[2]

Such a remark implies that the woman who sacrifices part of her career to enrich her life in other self-fulfilling ways is not really emancipated, that is to say, free. This means projecting onto women an already outdated, even grotesquely simplistic male model, in which only professional success counts, in which freedom is conceived as a lack of attachments, as an empty emotional life. If women choose to stay at home, it can only be out of laziness and inertia, not because they feel that their relationship with their children is an enrichment of life. Finally, the spectre of 'the housewife' is just a way of stigmatizing the act of 'looking after children', as if this activity were a sentence of imprisonment, as if it were an 'either/or' – while the majority of women today want *both* to work *and* to enjoy being with their children. Rather than stigmatizing women for what is actually a wise choice, we should, it seems to me, blame men for not imitating them by cutting down time spent on evening meetings and having to do office work at home. They could devote more time to interacting with their children: a highly rewarding activity.

It can also be seen in this context how pernicious another fashionable slogan is, one that suggests the need to 'manage the state like a business'. By this we mean that we should treat its various services as if they were for the sole purpose of material profit. We have already seen that this is just one aspect of a business, the other being the symbolic benefits that accrue to those who work in it. But the state is not just a service provider, it has its own symbolic power, it occupies the place of God – not, it is true, as an object of worship but as the guarantor of legality and one's promises. The state is also there to ensure continuity in a society: men come and go, the state remains, and can worry about the more distant future and intangible values. Beyond its functions of regulation and redistribution, it provides a framework for common life, which means we can place our daily actions in a meaningful scheme. With the best will in the world, private agencies, to which the state sometimes delegates its social service functions or the employment assistance it provides, cannot take on this symbolic role or add this extra meaning. The state's purpose is not profitability, but the well-being of the population. This difference in purpose affects administrations as well as institutions such as schools and hospitals.

Management techniques

The English word 'management' entered the French language a few decades ago, and generally refers to all the techniques of organization and management of a business, designed to make it more effective. But, in the neoliberal world of today, the term applies especially to some of its techniques that guide the organization in a specific direction. I schematically list some of them below.[3]

1 Breakdown of tasks

This practice has become famous since the early twentieth century, which saw the development of techniques intended to improve job performance; the words that designate it are *Taylorism* and *Fordism*. A 'scientific' analysis of the actions necessary to accomplish a task identifies the constituent movements of the action and their optimal sequence, which enhances performance and thus profit. But nowadays, these are not mechanical actions such as those immortalized by Charlie Chaplin in *Modern Times*, as tasks are now immaterial. We identify the characteristics of each act, specifying the number: the seven dimensions of this one, the nine steps of that one, the forty settings of the other. Each of these aspects is presented as an irreducible, elementary entity, and it tends to be given a standard form. The advantage of this practice is twofold: even though the analysis is arbitrary if not utterly bizarre, you can check the items successively to gain an 'objective' overview of each performance and, thanks to this appearance of impersonality, proudly point to the scientific character of the operation.

The techniques used formerly in factories are now extended to office work. Just by chance, I came across the management practices in the administration of a large local community in the centre of France. Although it is a public service, this administration is run like a business, that is to say, it is judged by the satisfaction of its customers – for, if the customers are not happy, the business is in danger! With this end in view, the business seeks four *certifications* from international standards organizations, a sort of summary of the usual requirements of clients, which concern: (1) the quality of the act, (2) the health and safety of participants, (3) the environment and (4) ethics. Each employee must ensure the compliance of his work with the certifications followed by his employer, and record the results in tables. In addition, each certification is controlled by another employee whose sole function this is ('Mr Quality', 'Mrs Environment', 'Miss Ethics'), and these 'quality references' are in turn supervised by two deputy directors, also full-time jobs. The compliance of the work carried out with the certifications, finally, is evaluated at regular intervals by an outside agency, an investment bank or an auditor.

This overall organization is complemented by a set of *values* to which all employees are expected to adhere, and which signs placed around the common areas constantly remind them of: (1) quality of service rendered, (2) respect for the individual, (3) exemplary nature, (4) commitment. Contravention of these values is tantamount to an anomaly – one that must be reported. Finally, on top of these certifications and values, there are *goals* for each employee, for example: (1) submit files on time, (2) address funding requests in a timely manner. Employees are encouraged at the same time to set themselves additional goals. If they accomplish their objectives 100 per cent, they can, at the end of the year, lay claim to a bonus.

This breakdown sometimes seems to have been inspired by computer games (or computers), where all complexity is reduced to a series of choices that need to be answered 'yes' or 'no'. If the operation is successful, we can well imagine that human beings will soon be replaced by machines, as has happened where they performed purely mechanical gestures that are easy to reproduce, as at motorway tolls. However, what we have here is anything but manual labour: this new Taylorism concerns the movements of the mind, not those of the body. As specified in the instructions that come with each certification, the latter sets out the requirements but not how to meet them, thus leaving 'a lot of leeway and flexibility for implementation'. The overall effect of this technique is the mechanization of mental operations: we no longer need to think, we just have to comply with a ritual. Its overall rationality becomes incomprehensible for the operators at the bottom.

2 Objectivity of results

This second characteristic stems from the first: through a breakdown of tasks, it is possible to remove all traces of subjective judgement. For this reason, the direct relationship between superior and subordinate, master and pupil, tends to be replaced by the use of tests where you can tick the correct answer, and by filling in forms. This last word clearly indicates the goal: that of imposing a uniform grid on all experiences. Moreover, by dint of filling in forms, no longer do teachers have time to deal with students individually, or nurses have the same relation to their patients. Contact from person to person is replaced by a solitary activity, and interpretation is replaced by impersonal description. It is as if the physical encounter between two individuals contained some sort of threat, because we do not exactly know what might transpire. This is what the American philosopher Matthew Crawford, in a useful book on the meaning of work, refers to as 'the distrust of arbitrariness'.[4] Threat is here eliminated, but, so is all the profit for the construction of their identity that everyone could derive from meeting others. Deprived of identity by this reduction of behaviour to encrypted elements, human beings are dehumanized. They ask for meaning, they are answered with numbers. They need personal recognition, they are reduced to formalized files.

3 Programming minds

The 'natural' programming inscribed within our genes is supplemented by an 'artificial', or rather social programming. Again, the metaphor of the computer is deployed. We can also say that 'the normalization of acts, which characterized the Taylorist scheme, is succeeded by the standardization of people',[5] what is sometimes called *Toyotism*, after the name of the Japanese car plant where the technique was developed for the first time. Then another boundary is crossed: we are not concerned with the skills of the performers, but with their know-how; it is not only their skills that are drawn on, but their whole personality. The distinction between professional and private life tends to fade.

If it is possible to format or to program people, you do not have to worry about their every move; the target is no longer their behaviour but their brains – which will manage all their behaviour. So what is demanded of each employee is a much more comprehensive commitment, one of his mind and not just his body; but it is a mind deprived of any initiative, trapped in a narrow frame. The individual must be, no longer a cog in a machine, but a link in a circuit. Everyone's mind is deemed to look like a well-programmed computer, becoming the interface between two machines, sometimes quite literally. In some companies, the employee follows on a screen the arrival of the data registered (e.g., the sales curve) and notes on another screen the necessary steps that follow (boost production here, decrease it there). One has the impression that, before long, even this minimal human intervention will no longer be necessary.

The unconscious model of dehumanization at work here is that of the *machine*, even if it is a very sophisticated machine, unlike the forms of dehumanization to which totalitarianism had accustomed us: Nazis reduced their victims to the status of subhumans, even animals, using them as guinea pigs for medical experiments; Communists treated their victims as slaves, making them work to the point of exhaustion. But these practices can also overlap with each other, since the end result is the same (it comes as no surprise to learn that Stalin was among the admirers of Taylor).

Toyotism conditions individuals, but does not deprive them of willpower: it does not try to make robots of them (like the characters in Chaplin). Everyone must first internalize the goals of the company, and, rather than simply obeying orders, must be able to take steps to deal with unforeseen situations; this gives the company's agents the impression that they are assuming real responsibilities. This indirect way of managing their actions is sometimes called 'governance', 'a technique for normalizing behaviour':[6] no fixed rules, but a conditioning meant to produce the expected results.

4 Concealed hierarchies

Yet despite this appearance of greater autonomy for each actor, and despite the soothing rhetoric of the absence of imposed hierarchies, the participants in the action do not have true freedom: their desires have been programmed, they now talk like machines. They are actually caught in a typical double bind: even though the dice are loaded and the objectives agreed in advance, they are forced to be free – required to behave independently. The constraint is invisible, as everyone has been convinced that it is in their interest to act in this way. Self-discipline replaces the rustic methods of yesteryear. Everyone is his own master, but the instructions are common to all. Injunctions are no longer issued by brutal leaders, but by organizations with no binding power: office for advice, training and auditing. The law is absent, but the pressure on each participant is even stronger as it is so insidious, ultimately even imposed by himself and his well-programmed conscience. Leaders no longer give orders, but the employee is judged from above (the management), from the side (his colleagues) and from below (the users and clients). In any case, the decisions to be obeyed are not presented as the product of a will, but as standing to reason, imposed by the very nature of things, by the laws of economics, the circumstances proper to each position.

While being deleterious to the social and psychological lives of those to whom they apply, management techniques only marginally improve business performance. Transposed into the world of administration, these techniques are no more efficient. The few benefits obtained are offset by the new costs they entail: six positions for supervision and control, in the organization I mentioned, plus fees paid to the experts in the external evaluation body. Filling in forms and tables occupies a significant part of the working day. One thus realizes that the imposition of these techniques, which is obviously not general but is an important trend in today's world of work, does not really stem from a concern for efficiency or profitability. Their purpose is ideological in nature: they are designed, in Saint-Simon's terms, to replace the government of men by the administration of things, to eliminate the uncertainties inherent in autonomous human activity.

It is just as if, in public or private institutions, it would be preferable to transform into explicit rules what normal human beings accomplish by themselves. In their previous lives, these employees drew personal satisfaction from a job well done, they tried not to endanger the health or safety of neighbours, not to damage the environment or accompany their professional acts with dubious jokes of a sexist or racist nature . . . They even tried to finish their work on time! Making their actions explicit and codified deprives them of their autonomy and reduces them to the role of an element in a circuit. The jargon used has the overall effect of masking rather than revealing reality, like the convoluted and hollow formulas of Soviet bureaucrats in bygone days. This 'normalization' is also a dehumanization.

Today, we tend to describe crimes against humanity as the highest level in the criminal ladder. The dehumanizing practices that are spreading through the world of work are certainly infinitely less spectacular, as they do not result in piles of corpses. However, they are much more frequent than those crimes and insidiously tend to paralyse the very humanity of those they concern, hampering their need for freedom, for an immediate relation with others, their need to contribute to the common good.

Several reactions have been aroused by this trend, and its particularly painful consequences, such as the suicides at France Telecom. Unconditional supporters of neoliberalism see it as one more reason for condemning the welfare state, which has spoiled its citizens by making them incapable of flexibility; it is because of their status as eternal recipients of welfare that they are so vulnerable when the going gets tough. Let them taste anew the delights of nomadism! The proponents of psychological interpretations have put forward the concept of harassment: everything is the fault of superiors who take a perverse pleasure in humiliating and persecuting their subordinates; the remedy is a more focused legislation codifying human relations in the world of work: those who harass others must be subject to prosecution. One may wonder if the problem, rather than being psychological, is not related to the organization of work and, beyond it, to the neoliberal ideology that underlies it.

A company that does not turn a profit quickly goes bankrupt. So it cannot be a matter of abandoning profitability in favour of the private enrichment of the staff, but of finding the right balance between the two. After all, a better social atmosphere is, from an economic point of view, beneficial to the company. But the state, through its laws, also has a role to play because it is the only party to act in the name of another logic, one which takes into account the long-term view as well as the country's natural resources, the health of its people and the need to invest in education. Today, in Europe, the only framework for effective intervention is theoretically that of the European Union. Unless such an agreement is made, the 'virtuous' companies of one country would go under when faced with competition from those which, in another country, sought only for immediate profit. Compared to firms in other continents, a moderate and nuanced European protectionism seems essential if we are to defend not only factories but also a lifestyle deemed valuable. Everyone knows, however, that on this point, practice is far behind theory.

The weakening of the field of law, the loss of meaning in the world of work and the dehumanization of human beings cannot be explained as just a conspiracy hatched by a few moguls in big business, although, inevitably, those who benefit materially from it do all they can to foster these transformations. The same is true of the new techniques of management and governance. These changes overall are the effect of a shift in society that was not triggered by a conscious individual subject. It is clear, however, that, although it is not a mechanical consequence of neoliberal ideology, these changes have been made possible by it, and foster it in return. These changes appear logical in a world characterized by a neglect of ends (the development of human beings, a life rich in meaning and beauty) and the sacralization of means (a prosperous economy, of which we do not ask whether it actually serves society, and which reduces companies to their market value alone).

The power of the media

I now come to a final form of individual tyranny, a tyranny that is no longer economic but social. In his enumeration of the powers in the state which must be separated so that they can limit each other, Montesquieu retains only three, following an already traditional division: the legislative, the executive and the judiciary. In modern democratic societies, we have the habit of adding two more forms of power: economic power and media power. So I still need to say a few words about the latter.

Freedom of expression is sometimes presented not as one value among others, but as the very foundation of democracy. One example led to much discussion of the matter, first in Denmark and then in the world: the cartoons of the Prophet Muhammad. We read, on this occasion, that freedom of expression was the 'first Danish value'. Should we, in this case, reject any limitation on it?[7]

That freedom of expression is a necessity becomes clear when we think of the isolated citizen, mistreated by the administration, before whom all doors are closed and who has only one course left: to publicize the injustice of which he is victim, by bringing it, for example, to the attention of the readers of a newspaper. But we are here oversimplifying our task. Imagine instead that the words aspiring to freedom of expression are those of the anti-Semitic Drumont, or are part of some hateful propaganda, or consist in disseminating misleading information. Let us also think, not of the isolated individual, but of the media group that possesses television channels, radio stations and newspapers, which can be made to say whatever the group wants. That these media are beyond government control is probably a good thing; that their action is entirely beneficial seems more doubtful.

While freedom of expression has its place among democratic values, it is unclear how it could be seen as their common foundation. It represents a demand for complete tolerance (nothing you say can be declared unacceptable), and thus a generalized relativism of all values: 'I claim the right to defend any opinion publicly and to denigrate any ideal.' But every society needs a foundation of shared values, and replacing them with 'I have the right to say whatever I want' is not enough to build a life together. Obviously, the right to waive certain rules cannot be the only rule governing the life of a community. 'It is forbidden to forbid' is a nice formula, but no society can comply with it.

As well as the freedom of choice that it grants its citizens, the state has (or should have) other objectives: to protect their lives, physical integrity and property, to combat discrimination, to work towards common justice, peace and welfare, and to defend the dignity of all citizens. In that capacity, as Burke already knew, speech and other forms of expression are restricted because of the other values espoused by society.

If one takes seriously these reservations on the absolute nature of freedom of expression, are we obliged to go to the other extreme and require the law, or public authority, to control everything? Are we doomed to choose between libertarian chaos and dogmatic order? I do not think so. Rather, we need to affirm that freedom of expression should always be relative – to the circumstances, to the way people express themselves, to the identity of the speaker and the person he is describing. The demand for freedom only makes sense in context – and contexts vary enormously.

Where do we express ourselves? We do not approach with the same demands a book we have to buy and read (rare and difficult actions!) and a newspaper article or a television appearance; or a satirical publication and a daily renowned for its seriousness; or a marginal issue on cable TV and the evening news programme. One small incident will illustrate this difference in relation to the image. In the autumn of 2006, a museum of photography in Charleroi, Belgium, organized an exhibition of work by a Japanese photographer whose specialty is to show naked women tied up. The exhibition was announced by a large sign on the façade of the museum. Some local residents protested, whereupon the museum director said that he would stick to his ground, and the censors would not have their way. But the disparity between the two situations, the photos in the gallery and the photos displayed on the street, is clear: entering a gallery involves a voluntary choice; to see the poster, you need simply be passing through the area. As for the contents of this exercise of the freedom of expression, imagine for a moment that the women were replaced by some 'visible minority', for example black people: a man may admit that he feels an irresistible urge to photograph naked black people tied up, but his exhibition might not generate the same enthusiasm. Finally, note the paradox: it is women who have been tied up who are taken to illustrate the claim of freedom . . .

How do we express ourselves? Debates and scientific publications should not be subject to any control: both because this freedom is the precondition for a search for truth (if we risk being punished for the results we find, our search is hampered) and because texts of this type have little direct impact on the public. We can therefore oppose memorial laws which sanctify certain past events, and refuse in principle to prohibit research on the biological foundations of inequality between races or sexes. (On the other hand, this research may be banned from publication as scientifically invalid by an editor – this does not involve any prohibition.)

The artist's situation is different. Contemporary liberal democracies believe that artistic creation requires absolute freedom – which is probably an excessive formula, because it assumes a sharp break between art and non-art. Or else it involves a singular devaluation of art: it is decided in advance that, whatever they say, works of art will have no impact on the life of a society. Paradoxically, totalitarian regimes which banned some painters and burned the books of some writers showed a much greater respect for their actions. The secretary of the Soviet Communist Party, Suslov, summoned Vasily Grossman after having a look at *Life and Fate* in manuscript. He considered the book to be dangerous for the political regime: 'Why would we add your book to the atomic bombs our opponents are preparing against us?'[8] Nobody wants to go back to that period and its prohibitions; but, even without setting up a form of censorship, is it not legitimate to discuss publicly the possible impact of a book or an image on the minds of its readers or its audience?

Freedom of public speech

Apart from these two particular cases, science and art, we still need to debate the freedom enjoyed by political discourse when it calls for more direct action. This is the sphere dealt with by the laws against incitement to racial hatred or to violence.

The most important contextual element concerns the identity of the person claiming freedom of expression and of the person who is the object of that expression. What matters first and foremost is the extent of the power they both possess. It is not enough to have the right to express oneself, one must also have the possibility, in the absence of which this 'freedom' is a hollow word. Not all information, not all views are accepted with the same ease in the country's main media. But the free expression of the powerful can have disastrous consequences for the voiceless. If you are free to say that all

Arabs are Islamists who will never be assimilated, and all Blacks are drug dealers, they in turn are no longer free to find work, or even walk down the street without being stopped and searched.

This problem is not new, and had already been identified at the time of Greek democracy. In this type of regime, it is the majority that decides what to do in public affairs, and the majority of citizens is not necessarily well informed: each person has his own concerns, he is not familiar with common affairs – which are often very complex; so he is willing to listen to the advice of more competent people. And those he thinks are competent are not necessarily those with a higher knowledge, but those who can talk to him in an attractive way, the masters of discourse: the sophists. Democracy is threatened constantly by demagogy; a fine talker may win the conviction (and the votes) of the majority at the expense of a reasonable but less eloquent advisor.

This threat of demagogy, already present in antiquity, has been exacerbated in modernity thanks to the ubiquity of the mass media: press, radio, television, and the Internet today. The drive to impose one's presence thanks to one's skill with words and images has not changed since those early days, but the instrument placed at its service is now much more powerful. From this point of view, the same applies to media as to armaments: our ferocity has not increased, but our ability to destroy lives and buildings is incommensurate with that of the Romans or of the northern barbarians. The movement is accelerating before our eyes: nuclear weapons on the one hand, and planetary messages on the other, received everywhere just seconds after they have been broadcast. Within a single century, the change has been greater than in the preceding two thousand years. Until then you could address only an audience gathered in a room or in a public place, or – a significant improvement – the readers of newspapers. Today, information is addressed to scholars as well as to the illiterate, people of any condition, from any country: moreover, it is instantaneous. Its sources are certainly many and varied – but that does not mean that all sources have the same power.

We believe that we make our decisions by ourselves; but if all the major media, from morning to night and day after day, send us the same message, the degree of freedom that we have in shaping our opinions is very limited. Our imperatives for action are based on the information we have about the world, yet this information, even if not false, has been selected, sorted, grouped, built up into verbal or visual messages to lead us to one conclusion rather than another. However, the mass media do not express the collective will, and we are lucky they do not: the individual must be able to judge for himself, and not under the pressure of decisions from the state. But in the present situation, he may also receive information that is as standardized as if it came from the state, but decided by a single individual or group of individuals. It is now possible – if you have a lot of money! – to buy a television channel, or five, or ten, plus radio stations, plus newspapers, and make them say what you want, so that their consumers, readers, listeners and viewers will in turn think what you want them to think.

Of course, the media mogul must also worry about the profitability of his empire, he cannot stick to just spreading propaganda; but nothing prevents him skilfully mixing this with other content that will sell (scandals, sex, violence). The end result is, however, that he no longer seeks to persuade but to manipulate; then we have, not a democracy, but a plutocracy: it is not the people who have the power, but quite simply money. The powerful individual is at liberty to impose his will on the majority.

I will take a recent example. The *News of the World*,

a weekly tabloid appearing in London and owned by
Rupert Murdoch's media empire, caused a scandal by
its methods of investigation and has been the subject
of a police investigation. We thus learned how political
power and media power were interwoven. The current
British prime minister, David Cameron, holidayed on
Murdoch's yacht; his director of communications is a
former editor of the offending newspaper. Its journalists
paid tens of thousands of pounds to police in Scotland
Yard, which enabled them to gain access to confiden-
tial information, but also gave them some protection
for their investigations that bordered on illegality. At
election time, all the media in the group, which also
owns several television channels, concentrated their fire
on their enemy, the Labour Party; the victory of the
Conservatives was heavily dependent on them. This did
not stop Murdoch from, at another time, having a good
relationship with Blair's Labour government, of whose
anti-terrorist crusade he approved, to the point that he
was publicly called 'the 24th member of the cabinet'.
His many services were rewarded in return with several favours granted by politicians in power. The same
media empire plays a leading role in the political life of
the United States, for example through the television
channel Fox News.

Another example of media control is provided by
the extraordinary influence these days of the Qatari
television channel Al-Jazeera on the political evolution
of Arab countries. This channel does not just provide a
wealth of information, but this is oriented according to
the political line that the channel has chosen to promote.
Thus, the fall of Arab autocrats was partly a result of its
stance; but it never criticizes Muslim religious authorities, or Saudi Arabia.

Public speech, one power among others, must sometimes be limited. Where can we find a criterion for
distinguishing good from bad limitations? Inter alia,

in the power relationship between the speaker and the one spoken about. A person does not deserve the same merit when he attacks the powerful of the day as when he designates a scapegoat to be handed over to popular resentment. A newspaper is infinitely weaker than the state, so there is no reason to limit the freedom of expression of the former when it criticizes the latter. When, in France, the website Mediapart revealed a collusion between financial power and political leaders, there was nothing 'fascistic' in the gesture, whatever was said by those who felt targeted. However, a newspaper is more powerful than an individual and when it indulges in 'media lynching', it is abusing its power. As a counter-power, freedom of expression is precious. As a power, it must be limited in turn.

It has been noticed that, in countries where the public media are controlled by the state, new technologies have opened up an opportunity for people to find things out – through their connection to social networks beyond any centralized control. Through Facebook and Twitter, information can circulate in China, evading the control of the Political Bureau. In the Arab countries of the Near and Middle East in 2011, the same form of news broadcasting facilitated the political upheavals. The individual taken in isolation is powerless, but sharing information has helped to topple repressive governments: no abuse of power here. In other circumstances, however, the same instrument can be used in the service of submissiveness: if all the members of the network dutifully reflect the views of a dominant figure, the result is a strengthening of conformism, not a liberation of ideas. What was a means of liberation in the hands of the dominated becomes a means of submission in the hands of the dominant.

In October 2010, a set of documents was released from a source independent of the US government: the WikiLeaks team. We learned how, during the occupation of Iraq, violence of all kinds, murders, rapes, torture and bullying were daily occurrences and how they aroused little reaction from the American civil and military authorities, which were fully aware of them. The reaction of the American government to these revelations was singular: it concentrated all its efforts on discovering the source of the leaks and the identity of those who had spread them, in order to sue them. The soldier Bradley Manning, the alleged source, was arrested and treated as a dangerous criminal, like the terrorists imprisoned in Guantánamo: he suffered harassment, humiliation, psychological torture. However, no word of regret was uttered for the criminal acts carried out by the US occupation forces, and none of their officers was indicted following the revelations. Contrary to what has been said, the 'leaks' of WikiLeaks had nothing 'totalitarian' about them: Communist regimes made the lives of weak individuals transparent, not the life of the state.

The defenders of unlimited freedom of expression ignore this basic distinction between powerful and powerless. They can thus sing their own praises. The editor of the Danish newspaper *Jyllands-Posten*, which in 2005 published all the caricatures of Muhammad, discussed the case five years later and modestly compared himself to the heretics in the Middle Ages burned at the stake, to Voltaire the sworn enemy of the all-powerful church, to the opponents of Hitler in the 1930s, and to the dissidents repressed by Soviet power. It has to be said that, these days, the figure of the victim exerts an irresistible attraction. But the journalist forgot that those courageous practitioners of free speech were fighting against the spiritual and temporal powers of the time, while he himself was defending a position endorsed by the government of his country and the majority of the population, and the target of these attacks was not the dominant force in the country, but a minority that suffered discrimination.

Setting bounds to freedom of expression does not mean seeking the introduction of censorship. Rather, it means appealing to the responsibility of those who have the power to disseminate information and opinion. This responsibility increases with the power we have, and should entail a corresponding restraint. There are fewer constraints on a book that sells 5,000 copies than on one read by 500,000 readers or a television channel watched by 5,000,000 viewers. For the same reason, a member of the government, let alone its leader, must weigh his words more than the leader of a party already known for its discriminatory and xenophobic positions. The rule here seems to be: freedom of expression must suffer fewer exceptions when the power at one's disposal is less, because then it is a counter-power; we must scrutinize it all the more closely when those who base their positions on it already occupy a strong position in the political or economic sphere; in such cases, it may entail an abuse of power.

The limits of freedom

Political messianism and neoliberalism comprise, at first sight, two opposing trends: the first shows the state's ability to intervene, and the second its gradual diminution. It is as if the force of the one compensated for the weakness of the other: the triumphal march of armies abroad contrasts with the powerlessness of the state on its own territory. One has the impression that, for President Obama, it is much easier to bomb Libya than to improve the social security system in his own country.

However, these two deviations of the democratic spirit (deviations that are actually based on that spirit's very own principles) also have a common foundation: it is a conception of man that sees him as endowed, always and everywhere, with the same rights; both are also part of the Pelagian heritage, imposing no intrinsic limits on their actions, whether these limits come from states or individuals. Political messianism therefore combines seamlessly with neoliberal doctrine, as illustrated in its time by the White House brochure already mentioned, which laid the foundation for the intervention in Iraq: human rights justified it to the same extent as did 'free enterprise'. However, just as we must restrain political messianism, which brings desolation instead of the development it promises, we have to place limits on the freedom of individuals.

The democratic principle insists that powers should be limited: not only those of states, but also of individuals, including when they take on the trappings of freedom. The freedom of chickens to attack the fox is a joke, because chickens do not have this ability; the freedom of the fox is dangerous because he is the stronger. Through the laws and standards that it establishes, the sovereign people has the right to restrict the freedom of all, because it can become a threat. The tyranny of individuals is certainly less bloody than that of states; yet it is also an obstacle to a satisfactory life together. Nothing obliges us to restrict ourselves to a choice between 'the state alone' and 'the individual alone': we need to defend both, with each one limiting the abuses of the other.

These days, we need to consider the significant increase in the power of individuals. Terrorism provides an extreme example. Technological advances make the manufacture of dangerous weapons available to groups of individuals. Before, only a state (and it had to be an especially powerful one) could organize an action as complex as the explosions in New York, Istanbul or Madrid; yet these actions are now the work of a few dozen people. Although the metaphor may seem forced, what is necessary to control terrorist individuals, that is to say an effective state, is as necessary to contain the actions of hyper-powerful individuals in other areas such as the economy or the media. Society must ensure a plurality of information with more vigour than it does today; a situation where the head of government is also the owner of many media, as happened in Italy, should not be permitted. The same goes for globalization: the economy prospers when capital flows and trade increase, but the economy is not the ultimate meaning of human life. It is the responsibility of society as a whole to submit the economy to political and social requirements jointly decided. It is not a matter of stopping globalization, but of preventing it from having adverse effects. From this point of view, we can see a certain parallel between human rights and the market economy: both are needed, and both must be balanced with other forms of intervention.

By definition, no organized society grants unlimited freedom to its inhabitants, since it gives itself a body of laws. The closest to this extreme case would be the country where total anarchy reigns (the word 'reigns' is not the most appropriate here: in fact, nothing reigns!), but has it ever existed? Such would be a country ravaged by civil war, and thus undermined by the collapse of all the central authorities. When Benjamin Constant wrote, at the end of his life: 'For forty years I have defended the same principle: freedom in everything, in religion, in philosophy, in literature, in industry, in politics; and by freedom I mean the triumph of individuality',[9] his theoretical position comes close to the anarchist ideal; but he is careful not to include in this 'everything' the spheres of justice and national defence. At the other extreme of this continuum, there are repressive and restrictive regimes both in the field of morality and behaviour and in economic activity – authoritarian and even totalitarian regimes. But, as is the case for freedom among anarchists, prohibitions cannot be all-encompassing, or all life would stop. In both cases, what we have is rather a regulative idea than a reality.

Moderate regimes still draw a distinction between freedoms and constraints, and this also provides a key to identifying among them those which lean to the left and those who place themselves on the right. Indeed, for the former, maximum freedom must be granted to behaviour: censorship, taboos, morality itself are all unwelcome. In contrast, economic freedoms should be restricted by state intervention. For the latter, it is the opposite: usually conservative in terms of morality, right-wing governments prefer to give full freedom to individual economic activities; this is also what neoliberal doctrine advocates. The left favours the free movement of persons; the right favours the free movement of capital. But, significantly, none calls simultaneously for both, as if restrictions on one level were needed to compensate for freedoms on the other. This differentiated approach also creates difficulties for those who practise it: it is not always easy to justify the lack of freedom in one area when you are promoting in another.

The experience of Communist countries demonstrated that an economy controlled entirely by the state brings stagnation and shortages. The recent banking and financial crisis that hit Western countries has provided us with an illustration of a complementary truth: left to itself, the market does not produce common well-being. We cannot count on it to regulate prices through open competition: this would be to forget the differences in the nature of the goods traded, products of work or speculation, and between the motivations that impel human beings, from the most rational to the craziest. However, the state is no substitute for economic agents. Its intervention lies on another level: it frames their practice by an appropriate regulation and, through redistribution, ensures the balance of common life. It can also contribute to long-term projects, of which individuals do not perceive the immediate interest, since their results will benefit only their children or grandchildren – such as ecological measures.

Communist doctrine interprets human existence as an inevitable and ruthless class struggle, the result of which, written into the laws of history, will be a classless society and the flourishing of all. Neoliberal doctrine denies the first claim, as it postulates the harmony of interests instead of conflict between them; but it supports the second, since it counts in its turn on the natural laws of the market. The collective will on the one hand, individual wills on the other, contribute to the achievement of these aims written into the programme, without any internal limit being placed on them. If we choose to abandon these providential visions of history, we can encourage freedom of individual wills, as did Pelagius, while imposing a limit to them, as did Augustine, except that this limit is no longer derived from the fateful phenomenon of original sin, but from the common interest, specific to the society in which we live. It is time to leave behind us this sterile alternative of all or nothing.

6

Populism and Xenophobia

The rise of populism

The people is sovereign: that is the first principle of democracy. However, like progress, and like freedom, the people can become a threat to democracy. This is made clear by the common contrast between people and populace, democracy and populism. What is at stake here? Let us begin with a short survey.

In recent decades, a new political phenomenon has appeared in Europe: the rise of populist parties. The transformation of the political landscape has accelerated since the end of the Cold War, as if the public life of a country needed an opponent as a foil, and after the disappearance of the Communist rival, the people had to project its fears, worries and revulsions on some other group. This group will be comprised of foreigners, especially if they are Muslims, resulting in outbreaks of xenophobia and Islamophobia. The immigrant, a multifaceted character, has come to occupy the place of the previous ideological threat. I will briefly mention a few examples of this process that has affected almost all countries in the European Union.

In the Netherlands, a flamboyant populist, Pim Fortuyn, published a pamphlet entitled *Against the Islamization of our Culture* and founded a party defending his ideas. In the aftermath of his assassination (by a young Dutchman) in 2002, his party won 17 per cent of the seats in parliament. According to a survey among the Dutch after his death, he was the most important man in the history of his country, beating Rembrandt and Spinoza. A few years later, in 2007, a new demagogue, Geert Wilders, made a name for himself when he produced an anti-Islamic propaganda film and called for the prohibition of the Koran. Since 2010, his political grouping has been associated with the government of the country (without participating in it): deprived of its support, the traditional right would no longer have a majority in parliament.

From this point of view, the situation in the Netherlands is similar to that of Denmark up until 2011, when the right-wing government was kept in power with the external support of the Danish People's Party, led by Pia Kjærsgaard – a party demanding 'Denmark for the Danes' and describing Islam as a cancer. In Belgium, meanwhile, the leader of the Vlaams belang ('Flemish Interest') has stated: 'Islam is the enemy number one, not only of Europe but of the whole world.' This kind of declaration is not without effect on day-to-day behaviour. I remember this little news item about an event that occurred in a prison in the neighbourhood of Forest in Brussels, when police officers replaced the prison guards who were on strike that day. 'On 30 October, four or five hooded police officers beat a detainee, took him into a cell and forced him to undress before clubbing him on the back and testicles. The prisoner was then forced to recite: "The Prophet Muhammad was a paedophile" and "My mother is a whore", as the report of the commission of surveillance noted.'[1] The Flemish press of the country called it the 'Abu Ghraib of Forest': might the case be contagious?

The xenophobic party of Christophe Blocher, in Switzerland, which hides behind the name The

Democratic Party of the Centre, uses its propaganda to liken foreigners to black sheep who need to be expelled from the country; in 2009, it successfully called for a referendum banning the construction of minarets in this fine country. In Sweden, the National Democrats, xenophobic and Islamophobic, entered parliament in 2010.

In France, in 2002, the leader of the National Front, Jean-Marie Le Pen, reached the second round of the presidential election, eliminating the Socialist candidate on the way; he won 18 per cent of the vote there. A popular novelist attracted some attention when he declared that Islam was the most idiotic religion in the world; an influential journalist announced that he was proud to be Islamophobic. In 2011, Marine Le Pen, who had taken over from her father, decided to play a leading role in French politics, and polls gave her around 20 per cent of the vote in the next presidential election. Germany, which previously seemed immune from these temptations, is experiencing a rise in anti-immigrant sentiment. In Hungary, the far-right Jobbik party spreads highly xenophobic (and occasionally anti-Semitic) propaganda.

In 2009, representatives of these movements met in Budapest, where they founded the Alliance of European National Movements, meant to coordinate their actions; its president is French. For now, these populist and xenophobic parties are not actually in a dominant position anywhere; nevertheless, they do participate in government, witness the Northern League in Italy, and are an essential support to minority governments, as in the Netherlands and Denmark. In France, large parts of their programmes are taken up by other groups; in Germany and Great Britain, the ruling right guards its rear by emphasizing the Islamist threat. If this development continues to follow the same pattern, these parties will govern Europe tomorrow.

This current populism is not a resurgence of fascism, let alone Nazism. Its historical sense is elsewhere: its current rise shows that a major page in the history of the twentieth century has finally been turned. The cycle opened by World War I and closed with the fall of the Berlin Wall, which saw the development and the collapse of the Communist utopia, the seizure of power by fascist regimes and Nazis and their disappearance: this cycle, which involved competing totalitarian and democratic regimes, has now come to an end. Of course, the habits picked up then are still with us, and we continue to hear calls to 'fight fascism' or to be wary of the 'unclean beast' whose womb is still supposedly fertile; but these calls serve only to help those who utter them feel smug, proving, in their view, that they are firmly on the side of good. No: the war is really over, and the new populism is not a revival of the utopianism of yesteryear. So we would do better to stop allowing the past to dominate the present, and try to observe the world as it is today.

Populist discourse

Let us now point out some of the characteristics of the discourse produced by these political groupings. In formal terms, their dominant feature can be described as *demagogy*, a practice which, here, consists in identifying the concerns of the majority and proposing to relieve them by resorting to solutions that are easy to understand but impossible to apply.

Sometimes the reasoning that leads to these solutions is misleading. And (I take my examples from the French demagogues) we act as if an analogy on one level could necessarily be extrapolated to all others. 'I prefer my children to the neighbour's, and the neighbour's to those of foreigners. So I am perfectly well entitled to mistreat foreigners and favour nationals.' This reasoning rests on a confusion between love and justice: of course I love my family more, but justice is the same for everyone. Or: 'Human races are unequal: just look at how Blacks win athletic competitions', with the subtext: and how much smarter *we* are! Here one first assumes that all individuals with dark skin form a single biological category, and we also act as if the hierarchy of physical performances made hierarchies of intelligence legitimate – a correlation that has never been proven.

Sometimes the solution proposed comes at a price that cannot be openly acknowledged: 'If I am elected, I will give more resources to the police, I will build new prisons, I will pay mothers at home a wage.' All these measures are expensive, yet the same demagogue promises to cut taxes. 'If I am elected, I will close the borders to foreign goods that compete with domestic production.' This would mean that other countries could do the same; but what if our country exports more than it imports? Demagogues refuse to recognize this fundamental principle of political action, in which every advantage has its price; they are willing at the same time to promise more security for all and more freedom for all, not wanting to admit that strengthening the one may well compromise the other.

Demagogy, as its name suggests, is as old as democracy; but as I mentioned, it has received a tremendous boost in the modern era through the mass media, particularly television. A newspaper is aimed at everyone, too, but we can at least stop, re-read the article, mull it over. The television news flies by, it favours sound bites, striking images that are easy to remember: our contemporaries, it seems, find it hard to concentrate for more than a minute . . . In this regard, the contamination is general: whatever the political message that we want to transmit, whether left, right or centre, it has no chance of being remembered unless it has been reduced to a memorable slogan. The form of communication determines its content: television itself is populist, and those who speak on television tend to become so. But this trend is particularly marked among extremist speakers. 'Three million unemployed, three million immigrants': the demagogue has no need to formulate the conclusion, he can count on the audience doing it – even if in reality the expulsion of immigrants would not put an end to unemployment. Television also promotes seduction at the expense of argument; the demagogue is favoured if he has an attractive or reassuring appearance, or beautiful diction, or if he can move people or make them laugh. Without a charismatic personality, populism soon runs out of steam.

The format of presentation of populism is demagogy; its contents come down to a few constants. Above all, the populist refuses to move away from the here and now, from particular individuals; he flees abstractions, distances, duration, favouring instead the concrete, the near and the immediate. While the ideal democrat tries to find inspiration in what Rousseau called the general will – a hypothetical construction of what, at any time, would be best for the whole people – the populist addresses the crowd with which he is in contact: a meeting in a public place, the many people listening to a television or radio broadcast. The democrat is required to defend unpopular values, to advocate sacrifices because he also cares for generations yet to come, while the populist plays on the necessarily ephemeral emotions of the moment. In the name of the general interest, the democrat is ready to intervene on behalf of minorities in the country, while the populist would rather stick to the certainties of the majority.

The democrat respects the law and favours ad hoc committees and study groups, where one has the time to weigh the pros and cons; the populist is at ease in deliberative assemblies where the handsome demeanour, the eloquent speech, the right word can win support. In 1968–9, leftist populism prevailed in the newly created

University of Vincennes: I remember all the resolutions passed on a show of hands in noisy and smoky general assemblies, where the most extreme position was always most likely to win. In contrast, it may be remembered, when Condorcet reflected on the system that we call democratic, he came to this conclusion: 'What, in every age, marks the real end of enlightenment is not the particular reason of one man of genius, but the common reason of enlightened men.'[2] This formula is a reverse image both of the neoliberal danger – the temptation to focus on the brilliant individual to the detriment of shared reason – and of the populist orator. Rather than seeking the advice of enlightened men and women, such an orator prefers to seek the immediate support of the crowd.

Big words and sublime ideals are here left to others; the populist claims to be concerned about the daily concerns of each individual. The dramas of other nations, and of foreigners in general, leave him untouched. Similarly, the solutions he proposes brook no delay, and the benefits of the measures he proposes should materialize in the next few days. For this reason, the populist prefers continuity to change, which is a leap into the unknown; he prefers to conserve rather than to reform. He favours order at the expense of freedom: the ordinary citizen has, in any case, few opportunities to enjoy freedom, when every day he can enjoy the protection of his space, his quiet habits and his identity. So the populist consistently plays on fear, one of the most basic of human emotions. He recruits most of his admirers from among the relatively less well-educated, who, not being familiar with many other countries, are against 'Europe' and against 'globalization'. His usual audience belongs, not to the class of the poorest, but to the class that fears falling among them and thus joining the group of the rejected, excluded and vanquished.

Compared to the traditional divisions of the political

field, populism says it is neither on the left nor on the right; if we are to believe its spokesmen, it would actually be 'below', with the mainstream left- and right-wing parties being rejected as unattractive, 'up there'. Populism is the opposite of elitism – if we give this term a pejorative hue; the rejection of elites means that populism goes against the democratic traditions that promote the formation of elites by merit. But populism is usually annexed by other forces, outside the central field of the political arena: the extreme left or, more often nowadays, the extreme right. This is why the Internet and social networks are viewed with so much benevolence by the leaders of populist movements: the dissemination of information escapes any centralized control and democratic consensus. In this way, the margins take their revenge on the centre, and extremism gets its own back on moderation: as it circulates, private speech has no need to submit to the usual constraints on public discourse. In France, National Front supporters are, of all Internet users, most likely to visit politicized websites.

Extremist movements identify, in the public life of a country, a particular person or group responsible for all its ills, and point the finger at it. Non-extremist or moderate parties recognize the plurality, the incompatibility of interests within the same society, and aspire to compromise solutions, negotiated rather than imposed by force. Here, the opponent does not become an enemy; you coexist with him rather than fighting against him. For forces on the far left, the guilty enemy is defined on the social level: it is the rich, the capitalists, the bourgeoisie; to heal society, we must defeat these enemies and make them 'cough up', or else eliminate them (as we have seen, Communist dictatorships implemented this programme). The extreme right is no longer defined by anti-Communism or by an explicit racism based on visible physical differences: that latter has been too compromised by recent history and the former has lost its raison d'être. Today's far right is defined by its xeno-phobic and nationalistic bias: everything is the fault of the foreigners, who are different from us; let's throw them out. From this point of view, and despite a few transient borrowings from Marxist vocabulary, a move-ment such as the Basque ETA is essentially nationalist and politically akin to the extreme right.

This is not the only effect of populist rhetoric, but it is one of the most pernicious; in contradiction of the principle of equality, a part of the population is mar-ginalized and stigmatized. This part consists of those who are perceived as outsiders, either for administrative reasons (they are foreigners), or because of their cul-tural characteristics (they are strange). The latter may be descendants of foreigners, or have attitudes that set them apart – for example, in countries with a Christian tradition, they practise Islam.

National identity

Populism has a direct impact on the political life of coun-tries ruled by traditional democratic parties. We find a striking example in France with the issue of national identity, highlighted by the government between 2007 and 2011. It was during the 2007 presidential campaign that the candidate Sarkozy, seeking to rouse the popu-list spirit, launched the idea of a ministry dedicated to its defence; once elected president, he kept his prom-ise. In 2009, the Ministry of National Identity (which could have been called the Ministry of Islamic Affairs, as Muslims were its main concern) launched a 'great debate' to shed light on this concept. Results did not live up to expectations, and the debate was suspended without any beneficial effect for anyone, except for the National Front, which saw its support soar. In 2011, the ministry in question disappeared.

To illustrate the misunderstandings that surround this notion,[3] I would like to take an example I know well: myself. I am one of the people who were born in a foreign country and became, one day, *French*. But what does this word mean here?

The idea of coming to France first occurred to me in 1962, when, having just graduated from the University of Sofia, I learned that I had an opportunity to spend a year in a Western country. There was no question of a definitive emigration; rather, I would be furthering my studies, immersed in the foreign academic world. If I chose France and Paris, it was because I was seduced by the image of a city that was a crossroads of art and literature. I was not the only one, obviously, and this did not make me French.

At the end of the first year of my stay in Paris, I had learned a lot. I had read many books that were una-vailable in Bulgaria, and gained a better knowledge of French, now the language of my daily life. I also made French friends – many of whom were of foreign origin – and, through them, I discovered several French land-scapes. Like many other foreigners in a similar situation, I prided myself on having become a connoisseur of French customs: I wanted to taste all the cheeses, and, to the best of my (modest!) financial means, all the wines! So I decided to stay another two years to take another degree. But this did not make me French.

At the end of those years, I had married a French woman and started to earn a living in France. My pro-fessional interests had evolved too. I felt increasingly involved in the public debate about moral and political life that was being pursued in what had become my country of residence and touched on subjects which could not be discussed in Bulgaria, since any public life was submitted to the edicts of the Communist regime. The great principles which were a lodestar in France, even if they were sometimes violated in practice, seemed preferable. The rule of law was superior to arbitrary rule and corruption, the protection of individual liberties better than the permanent surveillance to which the citizens of totalitarian countries were subjected, and respect for the dignity of all suited me better than the old patriarchal spirit or the privileges held by the new political castes. But all these inner transformations did not make me French. And there were many other countries whose citizens enjoyed the same privileges.

The acquisition of a new cultural identity is a process that can continue indefinitely. Yet the question 'When did I become French?' has a very simple answer; it just has to be focused on my citizenship – which, unlike my political choices or my cultural inclinations, is the responsibility of the administration, and thus indirectly of the government and parliament. This change occurred on the day, ten years after my arrival in France, when I was naturalized by a decree of the Republic. From that time, my civic duties have bound me to this country rather than any other, a counterpart to the new rights it has granted me. As for my private identity, it has certainly become a little French, but not only or simply that. I cannot forget the first twenty-four years of my life which also help me look at France with an outsider's eyes, and I attribute to the culture of France features that, for some native French people, are just (human) nature. Rather than being French, I sometimes feel that I am the resident of a single city or neighbourhood; at other times, however, I think of myself as an inhabitant of the entire European continent. What I am sure of, however, is that I do not want a ministry or its officials to decide for me what I should think, believe or love.

The Ministry of National Identity and the debate on the issue shed no light on it, but they did contribute both to making the integration of foreigners and their descendants harder, and to reassuring some of the indigenous population by pointing out who was responsible for everything wrong in their lives. Populism has been strengthened at the expense of democracy.

Down with multiculturalism: the German case

Since the autumn of 2010, we have seen another way of talking about the 'problem' of foreigners in Europe: this time it involved a concerted attack on 'multiculturalism', the coexistence of many cultures within a single society. The attack was led by the heads of various right-wing governments. The tone was set by German chancellor Angela Merkel, who said in October 2010: 'And of course the approach [to build] a multicultural [society] and to live side-by-side and to enjoy each other . . . has failed, utterly failed.' In February 2011, she was joined by several of her colleagues in other countries. The prime minister of Britain, David Cameron, stated: 'Under the doctrine of state multiculturalism, we have encouraged different cultures to live separate lives, apart from each other and apart from the mainstream [. . .] I believe it is time to turn the page on the failed policies of the past.' The prime minister of the Netherlands, Mark Rutte, spoke in turn of the 'failure of multiculturalism' in his country and the need to 'close the borders to the poor'. Finally, the French president Sarkozy added his voice to the chorus, saying that 'multiculturalism has failed' and that immigrants should be forced to 'blend into the national community'. How are we to interpret this unanimity of European heads of state?

In Germany, the debate had been ignited shortly before these interventions because of the book by Thilo Sarrazin, *Germany is on the Road to Ruin*. The author, a senior official at the Central Bank and member of the Social Democratic Party, was given exceptional coverage: *Der Spiegel* published five pages of the 'best bits' in the book, containing the most disturbing passages;

the popular daily *Bild*, for a whole week, offered the author a page to explain his views. The result exceeded all expectations: by February 2011, the book had sold 1.2 million copies, a quite exceptional figure. A survey showed that over 50 per cent of the population agreed with his views, and 15 per cent were ready to vote for a new party advocating Sarrazin's ideas.

The rejection of multiculturalism is not the author's primary concern. He starts out from two observations that he believes are supported by many statistics. First, ethnic Germans have few children, Muslim immigrants have many more. Secondly, the intellectual level of the first group is much higher than the second. 'We cannot identify any particular intellectual potential among Muslim immigrants. [. . .] The immigrants from the Middle East [he means the Turks] suffer from genetic defects' – and intelligence is inherited. These basic data are juxtaposed with an objective that Sarrazin takes for granted: it is better for a country to be inhabited by 'highly educated people'. In the current situation, Germany risks going backwards. The conclusion is obvious: we must 'stop immigration from the Near and Middle East, and Africa'. Rather than making them take intelligence tests, a laborious and expensive procedure, it is sufficient to check whether they are Muslims; belonging to this religion is in itself a proof of stupidity . . . At the same time, the immigrants already in Germany should be forced to leave. The rejection of multiculturalism is part of the measures that follow: Sarrazin does not want to hear Turkish being spoken in the streets of his city, and he understands the hostility manifested against women who wear a headscarf.

In the nineteenth century, Gobineau had a tragic vision of the evolution of humanity: the strongest races, he thought, always defeat their opponents but, as they rule over them, they tend to mix with them – and thus to be enfeebled. Sarrazin's intellectual schema is just as pessimistic: 'The cleverest people have fewer babies', he believes, so the advance of intelligence is compromised by the lowered rate of reproduction that ensues. Strength is in itself a source of weakness. This paradox is not the only weak point of his reasoning: many of its premises, presented as obvious, are more than questionable, such as hereditary intelligence, or belonging to Islam as evidence of a mental defect: no scientist can corroborate such simplistic formulas, which Sarrazin nonetheless presents as a scientific fact. If cultural traits are transmitted primarily by genetics, should the current population of Germany not worry about being the descendants of those pro-Nazi crowds? On the other hand, is it really so obvious that higher education is the only desirable quality for the well-being of a society? Should we not encourage the fostering of other qualities too (qualities in which the inferiority of the Turks has not yet been established!), such as kindness, gentleness, compassion, the spirit of fairness, courage, the ability to question authority? We remain puzzled by the ease with which his fans have swallowed Sarrazin's eugenic views.

Merkel's first reaction to these arguments was to find them 'offensive and defamatory'. But after a month, she may well have noticed how successful the book had been; herself suffering from a worrying lack of popularity as elections approached, she returned to the subject in front of young party activists. Without endorsing Sarrazin's genetic and anthropological lucubrations, she focused on what probably explained his success: the rejection, endorsed by much of the population, of persons with a different culture. Having announced the failure of multiculturalism, she went on to say that 'what applies here is the Basic Law, not sharia'; so one was entitled to 'make demands' on immigrants. The principle put forward by Merkel was made clear: 'We feel connected to Christian values. Anyone who does not accept this does not belong here.' At almost the same time, another prominent German politician, Horst Seehofer, minister-president of Bavaria, said that Germany did not need an 'immigration from other cultural backgrounds', adding, to drive the point home: 'We are defending the German ruling culture [*Leitkultur*] and are against multi-culti.'

Intentionally or not, German leaders were here confusing two orders of reality, whose separateness I have just noted: law and culture, the public and the private spheres. Multiculturalism is not a political project, but a given: any society bears several cultures within it. On the other hand, the requirement to recognize and defend the rule of law, the equality of men and women before the law, freedom of expression and the rejection of violence are all principles written into the German Constitution, as into that of most democracies, and it is perfectly right to demand that they be respected. The evocation of 'Christian values', however, has no place here. While many Germans are indeed marked by the Christian tradition, only a part of its legacy has been incorporated into the Basic Law, and this is the only part that can be imposed on all inhabitants of the country. It is not because a certain principle is of Christian origin that it must be regarded as binding, it is because it is part of the set of democratic principles that, moreover, are more connected to the Enlightenment than to any particular religious tradition. It is absurd to suggest that those who do not respect Christianity must leave the country: many ethnic Germans would be forced into exile!

Britain and France

British prime minister David Cameron has spoken about multiculturalism, at an international conference on security. The overall point of view he adopted was that of the fight against terrorism, and he indulged in a psycho-sociological analysis of why people become terrorists. The major premise of his syllogism was the certainty that every human being needs a collective cultural affiliation; the minor premise was the fact that British cultural identity has lost its momentum and confidence; the conclusion, that young people from the immigrant community, unable to endorse British cultural identity, turn in their perplexity to Islamist groups, which marks the first step towards their recruitment by terrorist networks. The rejection of multiculturalism becomes, again, a formula flaunted by those warning against Islam. It is true that Cameron surrounded his argument with many precautions and reservations: we should not confuse, he said, Islam (a religion) and Islamism (a political movement), or Islamic fundamentalism and terrorism of the al-Qaeda type. We should beware of over-general formulas, such as the 'clash of civilizations', he added, and agree to build new mosques where the faithful request them. But should we accept his analysis of the reasons that lead young immigrants into terrorism? The overwhelming evidence shows that the process stems, not from an existential vacuum, but from resentment born of the humiliation suffered by a group to which the young people in question feel close: in this case, British Army occupation of Muslim countries like Iraq and Afghanistan.

Cameron draws several consequences from what he considers as proven by his argument, presenting them all as a rejection of multiculturalism. With this aim in view, he establishes a distinction between passive tolerance, where the state merely requires obedience to the laws, and active democracy, animated by a 'muscular liberalism' that defends certain values. But the values he lists – freedom of expression, democracy, equal rights – are nothing other than the basis of his own country's laws, as of many others. Once again, multiculturalism is indicted because of the confusion between law and culture. It is true that, in Britain, there had been proposals to give sharia the dignity of law in some neighbourhoods – but this would have meant leaving the sphere of culture to enter that of the law. It is also true that in Britain, unlike in Germany or France, another meaning has been given to 'multiculturalism': not as the description of an existing state, but as a policy of active promotion of the separation of cultures, shutting the individual into his original tradition, and rejecting the idea of a common cultural framework. In this perspective, we can agree with Cameron's decision not to subsidize organizations that preach terrorism or even simply deny human rights, freedom of conscience and the sovereignty of the people.

The French president, meanwhile, expressed his rejection of multiculturalism during a television interview in February 2011. This rejection was in its turn quite enigmatic: if this word was taken to mean the plurality of cultures in France, this plurality has always existed and always will; if it is a case of active policies encouraging the separation of cultures, we would seek in vain for any examples in French history. The concrete examples of behaviour that should be protected against the multicultural wave are 'freedom for young girls to go to school', 'equality between men and women' and the prohibition of polygamy; but the laws of the Republic already ensure these things, and respect for them is required of all residents of the country. This does not mean that people's behaviour always conforms to these prescriptions, as shown, for example, outside any multicultural context, by the inequality between men and women both in the salaries they can earn and in the number of seats they have in the French National Assembly; but in any case, the necessary legal instrument exists. On the other hand, it is certainly regrettable that praying Muslims take over the highway (a theme echoed by the National Front), but the remedy would lie in building more mosques. If we think about it, we realize that the only 'culture' that is being rejected under the label of 'multiculturalism' is Islam; Jewish, Chinese and Vietnamese communities, though better organized, are never mentioned.

When, finally, Sarkozy stated that 'the French community does not want to change its lifestyle', one wonders if his opinion really reflects that of the population. The French way of life has changed dramatically over the last hundred years, under pressure from many factors, such as the decline of agriculture and the rise of urbanization, the empowerment of women and birth control, technological revolutions and the organization of labour. Direct contact with foreign populations is, in this regard, rather a marginal factor, and by far the most influential culture in France is the United States of America . . .

The debate about headscarves

We can mention two recent examples where the French state intervened to eradicate all traces of multiculturalism. In 2010 a law was passed prohibiting the wearing of the burqa in all public places, including streets and shops. Women who contravene the law can be fined. The French model has met with a favourable response in other European countries: Belgium, Germany, Switzerland and some Italian town councils had already planned to impose similar laws. In spring 2011, an open letter from the minister of national education extended this control of public space: women wearing an Islamic headscarf cannot now, unlike other parents, accompany their children on school trips.

The first prohibition is based on several arguments. One of them is that the full veil is a sign of alienation, and the women who wear it will be liberated once they remove it. We do not seem to realize the inherently contradictory nature of this assumption: how can we favour individual freedom by punishing a free choice made by an individual? One can certainly regret the existence of such practices, but by fighting them so repressively, we reduce the freedom of those who choose to follow them, rather than increasing it – unless we actually think that some people do not deserve to manage their lives by themselves, but that, like minors, the mentally ill or prisoners deprived of their civil rights, they must abide by the decisions of others. These 'disenfranchised' individuals are like those states that are not considered capable of managing their affairs and that, for this reason, need a military intervention by Western countries. Curiously, both groups are comprised of Muslims . . . However, individual freedom and equal rights are the basic principles of all democratic states!

Moreover, by prohibiting women from wearing the full veil, we will not necessarily free them from what is felt to be their prison; rather they are likely to have to remain locked away at home – and thus to be deprived of meeting other people who could influence their worldview. They are asked to 'become integrated' while being punished whenever they go out in the street, whether to visit a doctor or lawyer, or even to obtain a simple administrative document – whenever, in fact, they try to participate in public life.

A second argument concerns common safety: a fully veiled woman, they say, could hide a Kalashnikov on her person and carry out an armed robbery at a bank; or she could steal somebody else's child at the school gates. Frankly, we have not heard of any cases of this kind; but if you want actually to prevent such misdeeds, it is sufficient to regulate the few special cases where facial recognition is essential; there is no need to pass a law, the actual effect of which would not be better protection for banks, but increased stigmatization of Islam and those who practise it. And if the public danger of this choice of dress is zero, how can we justify depriving women of a freedom so basic that we do not even notice it: the freedom to choose one's clothes?

The ban on accompanying their children during school trips, which has not yet been made into a law, is based on a series of superficial associations. First we deem that, in a secular school, all visible signs of religious affiliation should be banned. We then extend the idea of school space to any activity organized by the school, such as visiting a museum or a garden, where we often call on parents to help; they too must eliminate any religious attributes. Finally, we see the headscarf worn by women as nothing more than an appeal to religious practices, and we conclude: no proselytism at school, so no mothers wearing scarves on school trips! However much they point out that, far from being a religious symbol, their scarves are part of their cultural identity and cannot be removed without shame, they are not allowed to join in.

The headmistress of the school that advocated a ban on Muslim mothers (and received encouragement from the minister) sees no problem here. 'A school trip is the same as school, and when we are with pupils, we do not show our religious affiliation', she said.[4] If we accept this hyperbolic formula, the question arises of why stop there, with school outings: should we not ban the wearing of religious symbols at home too, to prevent children knowing about their parents' choice of religion and being influenced in their future decisions? Do we seriously think that pupils who see a woman wearing a headscarf will be debarred from access to 'republican values'?

What we can see at work here is a 'muscular' or 'firm' conception of secularism. It consists, not in separating church from state, preventing each from dictating its choices to the other, while ensuring peaceful coexistence between different faiths, but in cleansing the public space of any traces of religious affiliation. In so doing,

we reveal an odd conception of what constitutes the
person: his physical identity is recognized, but we prefer
to ignore his mental characteristics. Now reducing
the human individual to the level of an animal in this
way is a diminution of his dignity: we accept him into
the common space only provided that he strips himself
of what he himself considers as his identity, acquired
during his childhood or chosen later, in interaction with
his environment. The secular individual we imagine here
is an abstract being, devoid of cultural characteristics,
even though culture is part of human nature. In sum, we
say to Muslims (as the same injunction is not addressed
to Orthodox Jews, Sikhs, etc.): we will be tolerant with
you as long as you become like us, in your personal
convictions as well as in the way you dress and the food
you eat.

Once again, the result of such bans is contrary to
that intended: the stigmatized mothers no longer feel
welcome at the school, they will not be able to convey
a positive image of school to their children; minorities
of foreign origin will yet again have to withdraw into
themselves, to stay out of the national community that
claims it wants to 'integrate' them.

As we review the arguments against multiculturalism
– accused of harming women, or of fuelling terrorism, or
of strengthening stupidity – we realize that the word is
being used instead of one or more others. We often feel
that the politicians of Europe have learned their lesson
from the professionals of political manipulation. The
terms of the debate are chosen, not by the vital needs
of the population, but in order to be able to attract the
sympathy of certain voters. We saw public controversies
in the United States focusing on problems of everyday
morals, such as abortion or gay marriage, rather than
unemployment or irresponsible bank loans. The debate
on multiculturalism, following that on national identity,
in turn appears to be a way of diverting attention from

other real problems (social and economic in nature), but more difficult to solve. It is true that, in this way, we win over at no great cost the fidelity of a segment of the population that finds immigrants to be convenient scapegoats. It is democracy which, again, suffers.

The off-the-cuff remarks made by political leaders about multiculturalism can have indirect tragic consequences, as was illustrated by the events in Norway during the summer of 2011. On 22 July, a 32-year-old man, Norwegian born and bred, Anders Behring Breivik, committed a double attack. First, he blew up a car packed with explosives in the government district in Oslo, killing eight people. Soon after, he went to an island not far away, where a meeting was being held for young activists in the ruling Labour Party. Once there, he began the systematic execution of all those present; by the time he was arrested, there were seventy-six bodies. A few hours before the beginning of his action, Breivik posted a voluminous manifesto (1,518 pages long), in which he explained his reasons and purposes.

In the eyes of this mass murderer, Europe in general and Norway in particular were threatened by a Muslim invasion that would rapidly destroy the traditional cultural identity of the people who live there. To halt the inroads of the jihad he saw at work everywhere, a dramatic gesture was required to startle and awaken the sleeping peoples: this was precisely the meaning of his murderous act. Muslims in Europe are too numerous to be eliminated by such actions, he claimed; but we must close the borders, then force those who are already ensconced to assimilate fully, and finally deport those who refuse. However, it is possible to strike out straight away at those who favour the 'occupation' of Western Europe: political leaders on the left (they are all Marxists!) and the intellectual elites who advocate multiculturalism and tolerance for diversity, those proponents of a politically correct antiracist discourse. For their crime, they deserve death.

We need to make allowances for the element of individual madness in this manifesto, and the inability of its author to draw a clear line between what he describes as a fiction and its acting out, between the video games of which he was a passionate player and the execution of real human beings. At the same time, this madness did not arise in a political and cultural vacuum, but echoed the discourse of current right-wing populist parties. Breivik himself was, for ten years, a member of the Norwegian Progress Party, an anti-immigrant and Islamophobic grouping, which at the last election won 23 per cent of the popular vote, becoming the second largest party in the country; he left because it was too slow and indecisive in his battle against multiculturalism. The manifesto is peppered with references to other extreme European or North American right-wing groups, which suggest that Muslim invasion is an imminent danger and Europe is turning into Eurabia; they call for a pitiless war (even if, so far, they have not found a document proving there is a plot, a sort of *Protocols of the Elders of Mecca . . .*). Wilders, in the Netherlands, became famous for comparing the Koran to Hitler's *Mein Kampf*, and the Islamic threat to the Nazi occupation during World War II; Breivik, who refers to him, was simply putting into practice the theory defended by the Dutch populist: must we not oppose those new Nazis who attack us? Other demagogues argue that antiracism is as big a threat to Europe today as Communism was yesterday: what would be wrong in an act of resistance against the new totalitarians? Finally, the leaders of the major European countries, as we have just seen, unanimously condemn multiculturalism or declare it to be a failure. Here is someone who has taken their words at face value! The similarities are striking between this lone terrorist and the Islamist terrorists responsible for anti-Western attacks, such as the destruction of the Twin Towers in New York in September 2001. They all seek above all to capture the attention of the general public by some dramatic act, and the justice of their action appears so clear to them that they are willing to sacrifice or at least risk their lives. They all borrow their arguments from fiery preachers who themselves simply utter imprecations, justifying them by the lofty goals they pursue: the defence of democracy in Europe or the reign of justice on earth. They all act coldly and with determination, preparing their deeds for years in advance: they become farmers, in order to buy the components of explosives without arousing suspicions, or they obtaining engineering degrees and pilot's licences. The obstinacy with which they carry out their macabre projects means that these declared enemies are as alike as brothers.

One debate can hide another

The vast majority of human beings need a collective identity, need to feel part of a recognizable group. Some individuals are able to overcome this need – but a whole people cannot afford that luxury: the feeling of belonging confirms each one in its existence. As long as the group remains more or less stable, the individual may not even notice it and think it is easy to dispense with. Yet the group need only start to change rapidly, or in particular to lose some of its previous privileges, for its members to feel threatened and seek to protect themselves – for instance by cutting themselves off from other people and keeping them at arm's length. So, today, indigenous Europeans have the feeling that their traditional identity is under threat. But there are different interpretations of this feeling.

Is the underlying reason for the disruption they feel

the increased presence of foreigners? Presumably it lies rather in the joint action of two far-reaching processes: the irresistible rise of individualism, and the acceleration of globalization. On the one hand, therefore, there is a dissolution of collective identities that are subdivided to infinity, with the common standards giving way to personal choice (a movement that spread throughout Europe from 1968 onwards, with sexual liberation, the retreat of religion and the collapse of utopias). And, on the other hand, there is an inclusion of traditional identities within larger groupings such as the European Union, or their disappearance in face of the globalized economy now emancipated from state boundaries (a development that has been highlighted, especially since the fall of the Wall, by multinational companies, relocations and the flow of capital). This twofold movement, of considerable power, is the common matrix for behaviour as different as the anti-Muslim crusade of the populist Geert Wilders in the Netherlands and the anti-Western sermons of the Salafists in Egypt. But individualism and globalization are impalpable abstractions, while 'foreigners' are there among us, easy to identify: they usually have dark skins and their customs are weird. There is a great temptation to see them as the cause of all that has changed around us, whereas they are only a symptom.

Another reason for collective concern is the evolution of authority in our societies, in some ways comparable to that of identity. The weakening of traditional authority is the effect of the great movement constitutive of our modernity: the affirmation of individual autonomy. Everyone wants to be judged by standards to which he adheres freely, instead of these standards being imposed from outside. The traditional rule can now be revoked by the popular will: abortion was a crime, it is now supported by Social Security. Religion is forced to abandon its role of providing us with social values. We know that in the twentieth century some authoritarian or totalitarian regimes wanted to halt and reverse this course of history by subjecting the individual to the social body again; but after causing untold suffering, this parenthesis is now closed and the autonomy of the individual is asserting itself more than ever.

In a democracy, we are all equal before the law, but the law is far from covering all the human relationships that comprise social life. The democratic and egalitarian model, transposed mechanically from the political field to anthropology, from public to private, conceals the hierarchical relations within society. Since 1968, it has often been said that it is forbidden to forbid, forgetting that there is no society without forbidding, without standards and therefore without subordination. The phrase 'all men are born free and equal' stems from a generous spirit and can serve laudable goals, but on the anthropological level, it is a falsehood. Men are born dependent and weak; they acquire certain forms of freedom and equality only by becoming adults. Political autonomy does not mean social independence and self-sufficiency. This mistaken view acts in turn on our world and destroys relations of authority a little more.

Where this erroneous view is the most obvious is probably in the relationship between generations: between parents and children (as well as between teachers and pupils at school – the two are linked), a relationship that cannot be conceived in terms of equality. In humans, more than in other animal species, the physical survival of offspring depends, for many years, on the lavish care provided by benevolent adults. The physical plane extends to the mental plane: it is through the internalization of the other – the adult, the parent – that the child becomes self-aware, that is to say enters the properly human. Finally, it is the love of his parents that gives the child self-confidence and prepares him to face the disappointments that he is bound to suffer in his adult life. Throughout childhood, the relationship between the two is asymmetric and unequal: the parent is responsible for the child, he has extensive knowledge and experience that he must seek to transmit, he gives without expecting any reward. He sets limits on the freedom of the child, allowing the latter to forge an identity; in a word, the parent has an authority over the child of which he will gradually divest himself, as and when the child acquires its autonomy.

Our modern societies are characterized by the gradual oblivion of the constitutive role of the family, often seen as a pure obstruction, useful only as long as you do not earn a living; and by the renunciation of this function of authority, particular on the part of those to whom it was traditionally attributed – fathers. The social equality between the sexes – which is increasing even if it is far from universal – is blurring the contours of this role even further. The situation is aggravated in cases where the mother raises her children alone. It is also more difficult in many immigrant families: the fathers belonging to the 'first generation' find it very difficult to learn the codes of behaviour in the host society, and they often have a very imperfect understanding of its language; they perform poorly paid work, of low prestige. So, even when they are physically present, they no longer have any authority in the eyes of their children. The disappearance of the regulative role of the family produces in reaction the – populist – call to strengthen the police further, build more prisons, and punish all offences more heavily; in general, to appeal to justice on all questions of authority. This is an illusory solution, of course: the police cannot replace families.

New forms of authority are being invented today. It is too early to judge, but one thing is certain: not to exercise any authority within the family creates more problems than it solves.

Relations with foreigners

Before the modern era, the world had never seen such an intense movement among the populations that inhabit it, or such numerous encounters between citizens of different countries. The reasons for this movement of peoples and individuals are numerous. The acceleration of communication increases the fame of artists and scholars, athletes and activists for peace and justice, thereby bringing them into contact with peoples from all continents. The speed and ease of travel encourage people in rich countries to indulge in mass tourism. The globalization of the economy, meanwhile, requires its elites to travel to the four corners of the planet, while forcing workers to go wherever they can find work. People in poor countries try by all means to attain the high standard of living of the industrialized countries, to find the conditions for a decent life. Others flee the violence ravaging their countries: wars, dictatorships, persecution, terrorist acts. These causes of population displacement have been compounded in recent years by the effects of global warming, and the droughts and cyclones which this entails. According to the high commissioner of the United Nations refugee agency, for each centimetre rise in sea level, there will be hundreds of thousands of displaced people throughout the world. The twenty-first century risks being one in which very many men and women will have to leave their countries of origin and adopt, temporarily or permanently, the status of foreigner.

Every country draws a distinction between its citizens and those who are not so: that is to say, precisely, foreigners. These groups do not have the same rights or the same duties. Foreigners have a duty to comply with the laws of the country where they live, even if they do not participate in the management of this country. Yet they do not cease to be men and women like others, driven by the same ambitions and suffering the same short-comings; however, more often than the others, they encounter grave problems and address a call for help to those around them. We are all concerned, for foreigners are not just our neighbours, they are ourselves, yesterday or tomorrow, according to an uncertain fate: each of us is a potential foreigner.

Xenophobia is wrong; it does not follow, however, that xenophilia is desirable. We must begin, indeed, by admitting that the presence of foreigners in a community can – also – create problems. It is not because they are 'Arabs' or 'Africans' or 'Muslims', and so on, but just because they are, after all, foreigners. Everyone needs to receive some social recognition in order to feel alive, and when he does not obtain it, violence can be seen as a way of getting it. Now the foreigner finds it much more difficult than the native to gain social recognition (unless he turns to his own countrymen, exiled like him in this new country): often he is unfamiliar with the language and cultural codes of his adopted country; he also suffers from the animosity of the natives who find his ways peculiar. So it should come as no surprise if the crime rate is allegedly higher among disadvantaged foreigners (obviously, not all foreigners are in this situation).

Often, this state of affairs is no better for the next generation, among the children of foreigners; even if they were motivated by economic or political reasons, the parents emigrated of their own free will, they chose where to live – unlike their children. The parents initially had a culture, that of their country of origin; children no longer have this, but nor have they acquired a new one: they are threatened by *deculturation*. Their vocabulary is thus reduced to the most essential terms for everyday survival, and does not allow them to grasp experience in all its complexity. In the place of multiple, well-established and differentiated forms of recognition, their only demand is for 'respect' and prestige: to have the most threatening knife and the most vicious dog, the best brand of shoes and the newest mobile phone. These young adults do not recognize themselves in the society around them and therefore are willing to destroy its symbols, even if these destructive actions harm them and their families: it is the cars of their own relatives and neighbours that they burn, the lifts in their own buildings they sabotage, the buses serving their own neighbourhoods they attack, the gyms for their own use they vandalize.

The danger that ruins life in the poor districts is not Islam or multiculturalism, or, in itself, the presence of immigrants; it is this process of deculturation, the effect of the dominant conditions of life. The answer to this problem, then, is not to spread the idea that all immigrants are potential criminals. The massive expulsions, decided on the basis of a figure fixed in advance, are shocking in themselves: they mean systematically ignoring the specificity of each case, and reducing humans to a number. Why send back to their countries of origin individuals who have lived in France for several years, speak the language, work, have family ties there? Why not take advantage of the fact that they have successfully integrated without external help and can thus make themselves useful to the country? They will do so much better once their presence has been made legal.

Living together better

The question therefore arises: what should we do to ensure that the presence of foreigners is easier for them and more beneficial for the natives? Every society is multicultural, as we have seen, and this as such is no problem. But the members of a society must also have common elements that allow them to live together. The first requirement of all citizens of a country, whether they were born there or came from elsewhere, is that they respect its laws and institutions, and accept its basic social contract. There is no reason, however, to exercise control over the cultural identity of all of them. In general, the culture of migrants, different from that of the majority, is destined to join the chorus of voices that form the culture of the country.

However, some customs, some elements of the cultural tradition, contradict the laws of the country where those who practise them live. What is to be done? The answer, in principle, is not complicated, although its application to particular cases may pose a problem: in a democracy, the law takes precedence over custom. If the law is not broken, it means that the custom in question is tolerable: it can be criticized, but not banned. However, no extenuating circumstances may be granted to 'honour killings', when fathers or brothers decided to punish their daughters or sisters by locking them up, treating them brutally, even putting them to death. Such crimes of violence and murder must be punished with the full rigour of the law, and the fact that they are absolved in some traditions cannot be accepted as an excuse. In other cases, special provisions allow a particular custom to be adapted to the circumstances of the moment (this is not what we chose to do in France by enacting a law on the burqa.)

A second rule of good coexistence between communities of different origins living in the same country is that they must have, apart from cultural traditions of their own, a common cultural basis, a body of knowledge on the codes that regulate life in this society. This is the role of education, in a sense that includes schools, but goes beyond them to include the political leaders of the country. Its aim is to produce a common framework allowing the multiple cultures of society to communicate with each other. The codes that are picked up do not concern moral and political values, which are plural, as much as those cultural elements that ensure access to the same social space for all. First comes language, whose mastery is essential for all participation in community life and for the acquisition of every other element of culture. This mastery is in the interest of the individuals concerned, but also in that of the state, as it will benefit from their skills. It would not be unfair to make the learning of the language free and compulsory for all those who cannot speak it: such an investment will soon pay off.

In addition to the language, the inhabitants of a country also need a common memory. The role of the school is to transmit it to them, but this is now complicated by the fact that in the same class, we can meet children from many different countries. Should we seek to improve access to their culture of origin? This is not the role of the state school, which aims to ensure that all possess the same culture, thus ensuring a successful social life. However, one can modify the content of what is taught. Students must learn the history of the country in which they live, as it will probably be the framework of their future existence, but they are not required to interpret this past as a pious story with the natives only ever playing two roles, blameless heroes and innocent victims. The opposite situations, which encourage a critical perspective on one's community, have a superior educational virtue. Western countries have waged war for centuries, they have also sought to dominate distant populations. Discovering how one's former adversaries perceived these episodes can be highly instructive. It does not mean replacing the rosy-tinted hues of nostalgia with the black legend, but moving beyond Manichaean habits that impose a rigid division of good and evil on everyone. This process is justified less by the recognition of cultural diversity than by the self-enrichment which it brings.

As well as what natives can do for foreigners, we must also note what the latter can do for the former, and what they already do, consciously or not. Immigration brings several benefits to the countries of Western Europe. Even apart from the fact that recent immigrants are ready to take on the trades despised by the natives, we know that immigration contributes to the necessary rejuvenation of the population, thus increasing the proportion of active to retired people. In general, immigrants are driven by the ambition and dynamism characteristic of all new arrivals, and have an entrepreneurial spirit and a capacity for innovation.

Unwittingly, they also render another service to the host population: by their difference, they allow it to see itself through the eyes of another, a capability that is part of the vocation of the human species. Indeed, it is the way we perceive and welcome others different from us that is our measure of the degree of our barbarism or civilization. The barbarians are those who believe that others, because they are not like them, are of lesser humanity and deserve to be treated with contempt or condescension. To be civilized does not mean one has a higher education, or has read many books and thus is very knowledgeable: it is a well-known fact that such achievements have not prevented completely barbaric acts. To be civilized means being able to fully recognize the humanity of others, even when they have different faces and manners from ours; we can also put ourselves in their place and see ourselves as if from outside.

The great religions of the past and present recommend that the individual should practise hospitality and help the hungry and thirsty, and should love his neighbour (who, according to the Gospels, is not the one who is close but distant). Such a recommendation cannot be addressed to states. However, their leaders should refrain from flattering primitive political passions such as xenophobia. In today's world, where encounters with foreigners are destined to become ever more common, we ought to make the most of these meetings, in their countries and our own, through cooperation and integration respectively. Our self-interest and our conscience both impel us in the same direction.

If I have dwelt so much on the place of foreigners and immigrants in a modern society, on their relationships with natives and the benefits that each group could draw from their encounter, this is because xenophobia and the rejection of immigrants are at the heart of the populist ideology. Driven by the need to find simple and understandable explanations for everything that disturbs everyday life, this ideology fabricates a familiar opponent who can be made to take responsibility for our misfortunes. Now that we enjoy infinitely superior means of communication to those of the past, in a world that has become unintelligible to the mere mortal, populists have every chance of gaining public support for their miracle cures, however illusory. They refuse to look beyond the present, prefer to ignore multiple points of view, conflicting interest, and the heterogeneous nature of society. While claiming at every moment to represent the people, they are diverting democracy from its true destination and, just like the followers of messianism and neoliberalism, they pose a serious danger.

7

The Future of Democracy

Democracy, dream and reality

During the winter of 2010–11, the world witnessed an unexpected event: in several Arab countries of the Near and Middle East, people spontaneously expressed their condemnation of the dictators who governed them, and their desire to see a democratic regime installed. In some places, the movement was successful; in others it faced fierce resistance, and the outcome of the conflict is still uncertain. But whatever the political destiny of all these countries, it is already regarded as established that the democratic model is now very attractive, far beyond the Western world where it was born. It is all the more striking when we see this same model, already at work in Latin America and Southeast Asia, playing a role (admittedly more limited because the opponent is more powerful) in China: Chinese dissidents are now appealing for democracy to be established. This preference for a political regime is not accompanied by any corresponding aspiration to join the Western world. There is an intense resentment of the latter in those countries that were victims of American or European imperialism and colonialism. It is particularly revealing to see their people aspiring to more democracy, showing that this is an ideal that is cherished regardless of its origin.

This aspiration has several ingredients. One of them takes the form of economic demands. The poverty, often grinding, in which a large part of the population of these countries lives has become especially intolerable since a well-educated middle class has come into being and, at the same time, public media throughout the country are broadcasting images of the opulence in which some local or foreign people live. Although it is doubtful that a more democratic regime will bring prosperity to all, the possibility of escaping the invasive control of the state or the tight grip on the economy by friends of the government is raising hopes of an improvement. But this economic concern is far from being the only one. We are also hearing demands for the rule of law, where the lives of citizens would be free of the corruption of officials, the nepotism of the powerful and the arbitrariness of the police. There is also a demand for basic individual freedoms: the right to express without fear one's political opinions, religious preferences and choice of lifestyle. People are calling for pluralism and greater media freedom, and a real independence of the judiciary. Part of the population, familiar with democratic institutions, is demanding free elections, a multiparty system and a limited mandate for elective offices.

These movements, which have been perhaps inappropriately labelled the 'Arab revolutions', have already produced one major result: they have shown that the populations of several non-European countries share the aspirations of the peoples of Europe; neither Arab civilization nor the Muslim religion prevents them from feeling the tug of democracy. At the same time, they have taught a political lesson worth pondering: this population will reject democracy when it is imposed by shelling and the occupation of the country; it will defend democracy, however, when it has demanded it for itself. So we have discovered that the way one attains an ideal may be even more important than its content.

This change, facilitated by the technological revolution brought about by the Internet and by the incomparable freedom with which information now circulates, recognizes the needs of individuals and peoples to have more autonomy, to organize their lives as they see fit. It is this social foundation which gives it the force of a steamroller. It is not at all certain, however, that the regime that will emerge from the current movements will be a Western-style democracy, or that this regime, of whatever kind it is, will be more sympathetic towards the West than the previous autocracies. Recent history has shown us repeatedly that a revolution can lead the country down a disastrous path, and a new dictatorship can replace the fallen dictatorship. Still, the very general idea of a democratic state is now seen positively throughout the world.

This sentiment was already widespread in the countries of Eastern Europe in the second half of the twentieth century, especially in the late 1980s, as I can testify: Western democracies attracted us both because they were more prosperous and because they ensured the individual freedoms of their people, they had established the impartial rule of law and granted a certain power to their people, who, at the next elections, could actually remove its leaders. In those days, our regimes also called themselves democracies – the word 'popular' was added, as if to compensate by the redundancy of words for the absence of things – but we thought that real democracy was elsewhere, and it remained our ideal. The differences between the old wave of democratization and the one we are seeing now are real enough, but they are on another level: for us East Europeans, attaining democracy meant joining the chorus of European nations – which is not the case in Arab countries today. On the other hand, the Arab countries are not controlled by a single centre, in the way we were all dependent on Moscow.

The faith we had in the superiority of democratic values was maintained by those who had in the meantime fled the Communist paradise and who, like me, had settled in the West. Often, indeed, they were the most unconditional supporters of Western values, as they did not hesitate to recommend absolutely any means of enforcing them in the part of the world from which they came. I still remember a stormy meeting in 1967 at Yale University where, facing a hostile audience, a Czech émigré courageously defended the US intervention in Vietnam. The biggest warmongers among the anti-Communists were former Communists keen to put their own pasts behind them. We are seeing the same phenomenon today: the most ardent supporters of Western military intervention in the Near and Middle East are often exiled Iraqis, Afghans and Libyans, victims of their own repressive regime, but sometimes they can be disillusioned members of the old elite. The indolence of their Western interlocutors makes them angry, and they do not hesitate to challenge them: 'How can you just sit there while my people are suffering? Do you think they are subhuman, not yet worthy of your democracy?'

I like to quote a phrase from Benjamin Constant, who, speaking of the private lives of individuals, says: 'The object that eludes you is necessarily quite different from the one that is pursuing you.'[1] This is his way of emphasizing that, in the world of human passions and desires, the position of an object is no less important than its substance. I am tempted to expand the scope of his observation further. Now that I have lived in the West twice as long as in my native land, I can still understand the reaction of my former compatriots, but I cannot accept it. Over time, I have also come to share the view of those who, rather than dreaming of democracy as an ideal, were born in a democratic regime, and who are not satisfied by the superiority of democracy over totalitarianism or military dictatorships. They often adopt a critical stance towards their own country – not, admittedly, by comparison with a supposed paradise elsewhere, as in the time of triumphant Soviet propaganda, but because they can contrast the real country and its proclaimed political ideal. They are critical, not out of nostalgia for a bygone era, but because they are desirous of a better future. We thus arrive at this paradoxical result, albeit one that is understandable if we follow Constant's logic: the democracy you lack is necessarily more admirable than the democracy you already have . . . It is true that the ability to submit one's own society to critique is one of the undeniable achievements of this political system itself and of the Enlightenment that inspires it.

As I stated at the beginning of this book, democracy cannot be reduced to a single characteristic, but requires the articulation and balance of several separate principles. Hence both its strength and its weakness: in itself, no principle is sufficient to guarantee the quality of the state in which we live, no goal is unconditionally good. For example, it is preferable that the head of the state, or of the government, be elected by the people, rather than being imposed by virtue of belonging to a (royal) family or thanks to a military coup d'état; and yet there is no guarantee that this will be the right choice. As a friend of mine said the other day: Chávez was legally elected in Venezuela, Berlusconi likewise, indeed several times, in Italy, Orbán recently in Hungary (the friend did not add: as Hitler was in Germany). Yet their political actions do not reflect any promotion of democratic values. This is true, but democracy has never claimed to be infallible, as was the case of the Communist regimes. Other elements of the democratic structure are supposed to counterbalance the excesses of a leader, which is why the three aforementioned attacked some of the basic rules: Chávez wanted to be president for life, Berlusconi sought to escape justice in his own country, and Orbán attempted to stifle the freedom of the press. They did not succeed (unlike Hitler), and this is a sign of democratic vitality.

It is precisely because this type of system is based on several principles at once that the hypertrophy of one of them at the expense of the others threatens the whole.

Thus, ensuring the material well-being of the population is a desirable outcome, but if the goal is followed to the exclusion of any other, you end up living in a world dedicated to the worship of money, consumption and entertainment. The overall wealth of the country can also mean that a rich minority becomes richer and richer, and the number of rejects grows. We forget in this case that the prosperity of a country is a means, not an end.

The peaceful intentions of democratic states, proclaimed loud and clear, would be a good example to follow if these countries did not, in distant lands, wage wars justified by the idea that they were bringing progress and defending universal values, identified today with human rights. However, for the populations who suffer the invasion, the sublime values in question are often seen as a simple mask which they suspect conceals the true interests of the belligerents, and these wars are no less disastrous than wars of conquest designed to provide the victors with more prestige, power and wealth.

Requiring that the people should be the source of power is right, but today's media companies facilitate the manipulation of the said people and ensure that the institutional correctives put in place to limit the excesses of popular passions are suppressed. Democracy is then replaced by a populism that ignores the internal diversity of society and the need to look beyond immediate satisfactions to the country's long-term needs.

Individual liberty is a fundamental requirement of democracy, yet as we have seen, it can turn into a threat.

Emancipation from traditional social bonds (family, workplace, regional roots) paradoxically renders all individuals the same: they ingest, all day long, the same information, the same ads, the same fashions; as a result, the rejected external constraints are replaced by an equally rigid conformism. At the same time, freedom allows one a certain power, and some individual powers lie outside all control and all limitation, contrary to the golden rule of Montesquieu. Today, political power is unable or unwilling to limit the economic power of multinational corporations, banks and rating agencies. However, the absolute freedom of the individual is not a desirable goal, and human societies must be based on prohibitions and rules that organize the communal life.

The feature shared by all these problems is that they arise, not from attacks from outside, but from the internal principles of democracy itself. As stated by the director Stanley Kubrick at the time he was working on his film *Full Metal Jacket* (1987), describing the Marines' training before they went off to fight in Vietnam: 'We have met the enemy, and he is us.'

The enemy within us

No illusion is more difficult to uncover than the one which leads us to believe that our way of life is better than that of people who live elsewhere or lived in the past. Today we do not believe in the idea of a linear and continuous improvement, though this does not prevent us hoping that we are moving in the right direction; as we have seen, this view was inherent in the democratic project. Yet, according to some observers, far from being marked by a process of *civilization*, our time illustrates a state of increasing *brutalization*, witness the cruelty of the twentieth century.

The situation today is, to be sure, less dramatic, yet

euphoria is not the dominant feeling in democratic countries. In 2011, in Europe, the main talking point was the crisis and European weakness, the inability shown by the states belonging to the European Union to agree on the policy they must pursue at a time when such an agreement seemed necessary, or the fragility of the young European currency, the euro. The heads of these states behave mostly as individuals within a nation who have chosen to attend to their own interests and neglect the defence of the common good. The hope of seeing Europe become a 'quiet power' is coming no closer to realization. In the United States, the influential Tea Party movement is forcing the domestic and foreign policy of the country away from any solidarity, and government intervention in favour of the common good is the object of suspicion. Like the Poujadists in France, over half a century ago, its supporters are demanding a drastic reduction in taxes and the abandonment of any idea of redistribution of wealth. President Obama, who nevertheless aspires to occupy a centrist, compromise position, is powerless to promote his reform of welfare or environmental protection, and is depicted by his opponents as a dangerous extremist (either a murderous Communist or an Arab terrorist).

'Humanitarian' wars arouse little resistance in countries that wage them and even enjoy considerable approval, becoming the norm of Western military interventions, even though they represent a resurgence of political messianism. Despite the crises it entails, ultraliberal ideology still dominates government circles in many countries. Economic globalization deprives people of their political power, and the logic of management, which leads to everyone being turned into a carbon copy, is spreading everywhere. Populism and xenophobia are on the rise, ensuring the success of the extremist parties.

Democracy has grown sick with its own excesses, freedom is turning into tyranny, the people are becoming an easy-to-manipulate mass, the desire to promote progress is turning into a crusade. The economy, the state and the law are ceasing to be means for the self-fulfilment of all, and are now part of a process of dehumanization. There are days when this process seems irreversible.

Living in a democracy is always better than submission to a totalitarian state, a military dictatorship or an obscurantist feudal system. But, gnawed away by the inner enemies which it has itself created, democracy is no longer living up to its promises. These enemies are less frightening in appearance than those of yesterday who attacked from the outside; they do not plan to establish the dictatorship of the proletariat, they are not preparing a military coup d'état, they do not carry out suicide attacks in the name of a ruthless god. They are dressed in the garb of democracy, and therefore may go unnoticed. They nonetheless represent a real danger: unless we resist them, they will one day empty the political system of its substance. They will lead to a dispossession of human beings and to the dehumanization of their lives.

We always prefer to think that what we condemn is completely foreign to us. The idea that we might resemble those we usually abhor strikes us as so unbearable that we hasten to erect what we hope are impassable walls between ourselves and them. However, without wanting to go to the other extreme, and to see all political regimes as the same, we have every need to recognize, as well as unquestionable oppositions, the frequent presence of a common framework. Like democracy, totalitarianism appeals to rational thought and science. Democracy should not be confused with either colonialism or Communism, and yet all three are often driven by a messianic spirit. This kinship was hidden by the global confrontation between totalitarian and democratic countries which dominated the history of the twentieth century. The Soviet camp, where the vast resources of a whole continent were placed at the service of Communist ideology, had become a real rival and enemy, which made it legitimate to insist on the differences: it was the 'evil empire', no more, no less. Its collapse at the end of the Cold War had the advantage of freeing its population but also the disadvantage of depriving the Western powers of a counter-power which acted as a brake on their aspirations to hegemony. They thereby lost a foil, a partner that (without meaning to) encouraged them to behave virtuously so as to prove how much better they were.

A similar reluctance to reveal any kinship with the enemy emerged in the aftermath of the collapse of Nazi totalitarianism. Since the end of World War II and the revelation of the crimes of Nazism, in particular the destruction and enslavement of entire populations in the extermination and concentration camps, Western public opinion has always tried to emphasize the distance between those monsters and ourselves. Even today, there is a storm of protest whenever a historian, novelist or filmmaker attributes to the perpetrators of those deeds motivations that we might share. People claim that wanting to understand or even just put into context the events of the past is tantamount to excusing them. Thinking that Hitler was a human being who shared certain characteristics with us offends us. This evil is terrifying, so we prefer to think that it is a monstrous anomaly, external to our history and our nature.

However, there has been no lack of minority voices to the contrary, even if we have less desire to hear them. Reflecting on the intellectual history of Nazism, one of the most perspicacious experts on the subject, George L. Mosse, noted that the racism on which it was based shared characteristics with much more respectable doctrines. Racism, he wrote, 'is not an aberration of European thought or a set of isolated moments of madness, but an integral part of the European experience', and it is 'associated with all the virtues that modern times have continually praised'.[2] After fighting in the Free French Forces during the war, Romain Gary sought to reveal, from his first books onwards, the humanity of the enemy or, what comes down to the same thing, our own inhumanity. In his novel *Tulip*, published in 1946, Uncle Nat, a Black from Harlem, said: 'What is criminal in the German, is Man.' Later, in *The Good Half*, the Algerian Raton tells his friend Luke: 'You know how many Krauts there are in the world? Three billion.'[3] For Gary, it is not only modern times that we need to think of when explaining Nazism, but the whole history of mankind.

Discovering the enemy within us is much more disturbing than thinking he is far away from us, and completely different. As long as democracy had a hideous enemy, Nazi or Communist totalitarianism, it ignored its internal threats; today, it is forced to confront them. What are its chances of overcoming them?

I do not believe that radical change is possible (or indeed desirable), or that a revolution would solve all problems. The current transformations in democracy are the effect neither of a conspiracy nor of some malicious intent, which is why they are difficult to stop. They come from a change of mentality, which in turn is linked to a series of multiple, anonymous and underground changes, ranging from technology to demographics via geopolitics. The promotion of the individual, the new autonomy of the economy and the commercialism of society cannot be repealed by a decree of the National Assembly, or by storming a new Bastille. The experience of totalitarian regimes is there to remind us that if we ignore these great historical trends, we inevitably head towards disaster. I do not believe that salvation lies in some technological innovation that would make life easier for all. Technology made exceptional progress in the past century, allowing us to control matter ever more effectively, but these advances themselves have produced a surprising result: the awareness that no technology will ever meet all our expectations. It is not enough to keep improving the instruments, we must also ask what goals we want to achieve. In what kind of world do we want to live? What kind of life do we want to lead?

So I do not believe in any of these radical solutions. Such reluctance sometimes leads to resignation, cynicism or the kind of nihilism that has been baptised *néantisme*[4] – the conviction that all human actions are futile and that the world is going to ruin. This, however, is not my case. If I try to determine the sources of this, after all, positive frame of mind, I find them (apart from my own possible naivety) in the daily behaviour of the individuals I meet. Selfish, authoritarian and malicious acts are not in short supply, but I also see these individuals being inspired by love for and devotion to others, near and far, by the passion for knowledge and truth and the need to create meaning and beauty around them. These impulses do not relate only to private life and arise from anthropological traits inherent in our species, and can be found in certain institutions and social projects, thanks to which every inhabitant in the country can benefit from the system of justice, healthcare, public education and the social services.

I do not know how the energy reflected in such activities may contribute to reversing the trends of the current politics, but I cannot imagine that such energy will remain forever without consequences.

Towards renewal?

Rather than seeking a cure for our ills in a political or technological revolution, I would look for it in a new change of mentality that would allow us to recover the

sense of the democratic project and to balance its principles better: the power of the people, faith in progress,
individual freedoms, market economy, natural rights,
the sacredness of the human sphere. We can observe
around us various signs of the need for these, such as
the debates triggered by the recent financial crisis (they
were not followed by any concrete action, but at least
the fundamental questions were formulated) and technological accidents (like Fukushima). Or, on a quite
different level, the street protests in several Western
countries, such as Spain and Greece, organized by the
indignados, these young people who ask not to replace
democracy by another regime, but to bring it closer to
reality: 'Democracy now!' These are spontaneous movements, barely articulated, not able to formulate concrete
proposals, and yet their meaning appears quite clearly:
they reject the neoliberal turn taken by the governments
of those countries. We cannot yet know what will be
the result, a regeneration of democracy or a surge of
populism, but it is clear that they express dissatisfaction
with the system as it works now.

The goals of political action do not follow from
knowledge of the world, contrary to what the partisans
of scientism used to argue. However, if we fail to understand the society in which we live, we may make bad
mistakes. This is why it is desirable to take account of
what we learn from the humanities and the social sciences
about the characteristics of the individual and collective
lives of human beings. Here, realism is not opposed to
idealism or to policies inspired by moral goals, but it
moves beyond the pairs formed by conservative inaction
and blind voluntarism, passive resignation and naïve
daydreaming. Such a realism alone is the vocation of the
politician. We cannot think properly about the future of
democracy if we believe that the desire for wealth is the
supreme good of the human being, or social life is just
one choice among others, an optional extra.

In recent years, we have seen the development of an ecological mind-set that is not opposed to science, but wants to replace a very partial science with another, more comprehensive version, taking into account not only human beings but also the natural environment in which they live. This ecology of nature must in turn be made complete. To quote again from Flahault:

> Ecology as we know it today is still a restricted ecology since it only takes into consideration the human being as a physical organism living on earth. A generalized ecology views culture and society in the way that ecology already views our physical environment; it is interested in the conditions of psychic existence, its vulnerability and the vulnerability of social ecosystems.[5]

Cultural belonging and life in society are part of human nature.

It is within such a social and political ecology that we can take into account the complementarity between individual and community, economic goals and the aspiration to meaning, the desire for independence and the need for attachment. It is in this context that we can also see why we must resist the consequences of neoliberalism, such as the systematic replacement of law with contracts, dehumanizing management techniques and the quest for immediate maximum profit. Here too we can consider the advantages and disadvantages of cultural diversity and the imposition of the same moral values on all.

If we turn to the world stage, and not just that of the state, the lessons of the ecology of nature should again be complemented by those of social ecology. The first warns us that the world's population is continuing to grow, and people in many countries now have the means to raise their standard of living, even though the earth's resources in energy, water and fertile land are limited. The second tells us that the time of the global

hegemony of one country or even one group of countries is over, that the humiliation inflicted on others
by arrogant policies leads to lasting resentment and its
adverse consequences, that one cannot impose the good
on others, even when we are sincerely convinced of our
superiority (as shown clearly by the turbulent destiny
of democracy in the Middle East). This means that we
have entered a multipolar world where negotiation and
the quest for shared interests produce better results than
domination, even if this is exercised in the name of the
good. This new perspective on international relations
does not, however, lead us to conclude, like Bastiat,
that we are moving slowly towards universal harmony:
group interests still diverge, aggression is always possible, and a defence capability thus remains necessary.

I would like to think that this democratic renewal
will find a propitious place in the continent that saw
the birth of this type of regime: Europe. It is easy to
understand why the framework of the European Union
is preferable to that of the nation-states of the continent
itself, which still dominated the world a hundred years
ago, on the eve of World War I: these states today have
become too weak to be able to influence the process of
globalization in the way they see fit, or to play an active
role in the world. But Europe also has some advantages
with which to impress other countries of imposing
dimensions, continent-sized countries such as China,
India, Russia, the United States and Brazil. It is true
that, in order to realize this, we must take a step back
from current affairs. The advantages of Europe are so
far only potential – but they are no less real. And it may
be that the European tortoise will one day overtake the
hares that are at present running ahead of it – especially
if it turns out that they have not been going the right
way . . .

These benefits can be reduced essentially to a long
practice of pluralism: the pluralism of ethnic groups,

very different from each other because of the very nature of the land they live in, separated from each other by seas and high mountains, but forced to socialize with one another; the pluralism of families of thought that, since ancient times, have confronted and influenced one another: sophists and Platonists, Orthodox Christians and heretics, humanists and anti-humanists, liberals and socialists ... This practice of pluralism has been, as we know, tragically insufficient to prevent the massacres that have bloodied these lands; nevertheless, it has helped to form a set of values that should help us oppose the various forms of dehumanization that now range from programming people's brains to Toyotizing their behaviour.

These characteristics of the peoples of Europe are not sufficient to remove the deviations of democracy – messianism, ultraliberalism and populism – but they do comprise a site for resistance. If only Europe were able to seize this opportunity of giving democracy a new foundation, it would help to perfect a model that would enable it to emerge from the sterile opposition between repressive patriarchal society and dehumanized ultraliberal society, a model that other countries would be glad to follow elsewhere in the world. We can start to dream of a 'European Spring', coming after the 'Arab Spring', that would restore its full meaning to the democratic adventure that started a few hundred years ago. Has the time not come to hear and implement the contemporary call: 'Democracy now'?

We are, all of us inhabitants of the earth, now engaged in the same adventure, obliged to succeed or fail together. Although each individual is powerless before the enormity of the challenges, the fact remains: history does not obey immutable laws, Providence does not decide our destiny, and the future depends on the will of individuals.

Notes

Chapter 1 Democracy and its Discontents

1 Herodotus, *The History*, tr. G. C. Macaulay, VII, 10: available at http://www.gutenberg.org/files/2456/ 2456-h/2456-h.htm#link72H_4_0001, accessed 27 March 2014.

Chapter 2 An Ancient Controversy

1 My reading of this historical episode owes much to P. Brown, *Augustine of Hippo: A Biography* (Berkeley and Los Angeles: University of California Press, 2000) and F. Flahault, *Adam et Ève: La condition humaine* (Paris: Mille et une nuits, 2007).
2 Quotations from Pelagius are taken from B. R. Rees, *Pelagius: Life and Letters* (Woodbridge: Boydell Press, 1998).
3 F. Dolbeau, 'Le sermon 348A de Saint Augustin contre Pélage', *Recherches augustiniennes*, 28 (1995), p. 40.
4 Quotations from the *Confessions* of St Augustine are taken from the translation by E. B. Pusey, available at http://www.gutenberg.org/files/3296/3296-h/3296-h. htm#link2H_4_0010, accessed 27 March 2014.

5　B. Pascal, *Pensées*, Brunschvicg fragment no. 430, tr. W. F. Trotter, available at http://www.gutenberg. org/files/18269/18269-h/18269–h.htm, accessed 27 March 2014.

6　L. Dumont, *Essais sur l'individualisme* (Paris: Le Seuil, 1983), pp. 59–67.

7　Pico della Mirandola, *Oration on the Dignity of Man*, available at http://vserver1.cscs.lsa.umich.edu/ ~crshalizi/Mirandola; Erasmus, *On the Freedom of the Will*, tr. and ed. E. G. Rupp, in collaboration with A. N. Marlow, in *Luther and Erasmus: Free Will and Salvation*, ed. E. G. Rupp and P. S. Watson (London: SCM Press, 1969), p. 81; M. de Montaigne, *Essays*, tr. C. Cotton, I, 28, and I, 26, available at http://www.gutenberg.org/files/3600/ 3600-h/3600–h.htm, accessed 27 March 2014.

8　R. Descartes, *The Passions of the Soul*, tr. J. Bennett, 152, available at http://www.earlymoderntexts.com/ pdfs/descartes1649.pdf, accessed 27 March 2014.

9　Montesquieu, *The Spirit of Laws*, I, 1, and XI, 6, available at http://www.constitution.org/cm/sol.txt, accessed 27 March 2014.

10　J.-J. Rousseau, *The Social Contract*, tr. J. Bennett, I, 4, available at http://www.earlymoderntexts.com/ pdfs/rousseau1762.pdf, accessed 27 March 2014; 'Letter to Beaumont', in *Letter to Beaumont, Letters Written from the Mountain, and Related Writings*, tr. C. Kelly and J. R. Bush, ed. C. Kelly and E. Grace (Hanover, NH: University of New England Press, 2001), p. 48.

11　Montesquieu, *The Spirit of Laws*, XI, 4.

12　J.-J. Rousseau, *On the Origin of Language*, in *On the Origin of Language. Two Essays: Jean-Jacques Rousseau and Johann Gottfried Herder*, tr., with afterwords, J. H. Moran and A. Gode (Chicago: University of Chicago Press, 1966), p. 32; *A Discourse upon the Origin and the Foundation of*

the *Inequality among Mankind*, available at http:/
/www.gutenberg.org/cache/epub/11136/pg11136.
html, accessed 27 March 2014; 'Lettre sur la vertu,
l'individu et la société', *Annales de la société Jean-
Jacques Rousseau*, XLI (1997), p. 325.

Chapter 3 Political Messianism

1 R. Saint-Étienne, *Considérations sur les intérêts
du Tiers-État*, 2nd edn (Paris: no pub., 1788),
p. 13.
2 Saint-Just, *Discours sur la Constitution à donner à
la France*, 24 April 1793, in *Oeuvres* (Paris: no pub.,
1834), p. 74.
3 Condorcet, *Cinq mémoires sur l'instruction pub-
lique* (Paris: GF-Flammarion, 1994).
4 Quotation taken from D. A. Bell, *The First Total
War: Napoleon's Europe and the Birth of Modern
Warfare* (London: Bloomsbury, 2008), p. 144. I
here follow Bell's analysis.
5 Bell, *The First Total War*, p. 115.
6 Bell, *The First Total War*, pp. 143, 180, 182.
7 Bell, *The First Total War*, pp. 201, 276.
8 Bell, *The First Total War*, p. 287.
9 Condorcet, *Outlines of an Historical View of the
Progress of the Human Mind*, available at http:/
/oll.libertyfund.org/titles/condorcet-outlines-of-an-
historical-view-of-the-progress-of-the-human-mind,
accessed 27 March 2014.
10 Quoted by L. Febvre, 'Civilisation, évolution d'un
mot et d'un groupe d'idées', in *Civilisation, le mot et
l'idée* (Paris: La Renaissance du livre, 1930), p. 47;
Bell, *The First Total War*, p. 214.
11 J. Ferry, speech given on 28 July 1885, in *Discours
et opinions*, 7 vols., vol. I (Paris: no pub., 1885), pp.
210–11.

12 F. Furet, *La Révolution* (Paris: Hachette, 1988), vol. I, p. 309.
13 Bell, *The First Total War*, p. 390.
14 K. Marx and F. Engels, *Manifesto of the Communist Party*, available at http://www.gutenberg.org/cache/epub/61/pg61.html, accessed 27 March 2014.
15 Marx and Engels, *Manifesto of the Communist Party*.
16 Cf. M. Malia, *History's Locomotives: Revolutions and the Making of the Modern World* (New Haven, CT: Yale University Press, 2006), p. 148.
17 I have analysed this in more detail in my book *Hope and Memory: Reflections on the Twentieth Century*, tr. D. Bellos (London: Atlantic Books, 2005), pp. 237ff; see also the original French version, *Mémoire du mal, tentation du bien*, now republished in *Le Siècle des totalitarismes* (Paris: Robert Laffont, 'Bouquins', 2010), pp. 783–842.
18 C. Péguy, *L'Argent suite* (Paris: no pub., 1913), p. 149.
19 I have written two books on the Iraq war and its consequences: *The New World Disorder*, tr. A. Brown (Cambridge: Polity, 2004) and *The Fear of Barbarians*, tr. A. Brown (Cambridge: Polity, 2010).
20 H. D. S. Greenway, 'Fatal combination of hubris and incompetence', *Boston Globe*, 3 September 2003; M. Scheuer, *Imperial Hubris: Why the West is Losing the War on Terror* (Washington, DC: Potomak, 2005); M. Issikoff and D. Corn, *Hubris: The Inside Story of Spin, Scandal, and the Selling of the Iraq War* (New York: Crown, 2006); D. Owen, *The Hubris Syndrome: Bush, Blair and the Intoxication of Power* (London: Politico's, 2007).
21 S. Portelli, 'Les mots, première dérive, premier combat', *Mémoires*, no. 53 (2011), p. 8.
22 M. T. Flynn, *Fixing Intel: A Blueprint for Making Intelligence Relevant in Afghanistan* (Washington,

DC: Center for a New American Century, 2010), p. 8.
23 Cf. *Le Monde*, 13–14 March 2011.
24 Pascal, *Pensées*, 358.

Chapter 4 The Tyranny of Individuals

1 B. Constant, *Principes de politique applicables à tous les gouvernements* (Geneva: Droz, 1980), II, 1, p. 49.
2 Constant, *Principes de politique*, II, 6, p. 58; XII, 1, p. 275.
3 L. Dumont, *Homo aequalis* (Paris: Gallimard, 1977), p. 15.
4 Helvétius, *De l'Esprit, or Essays on the Mind*, tr. W. Mudford (London: M. Jones, 1807), p. xxxi.
5 B. Constant, 'Additions' (1810) to the *Principes de politique*, p. 531.
6 Cf. F. Flahault, *Le Crépuscule de Prométhée* (Paris: Mille et une nuits, 2008), pp. 60–76.
7 J.-J. Rousseau, *Émile*, tr. B. Foxley (n.p.: Floating Press, 2009), p. 108.
8 B. Constant, *Commentaire sur l'ouvrage de Filangieri* (Paris: Les Belles-lettres, 2004), I, 7, pp. 51–2.
9 Constant, *Filangieri*, I, 7, pp. 53–4; II, 11, p. 186; II, 9, p. 176; IX, 6, p. 332.
10 The works of Bastiat are freely accessible online: see for example http://www.gutenberg.org/files/44800/44800-h/44800–h.htm, accessed 27 March 2014.
11 On the thought and personality of Ayn Rand, see the chapter 'Prométhée, version ultralibérale' in Flahault, *Le crépuscule de Prométhée*, pp. 183–236.
12 Flahault, *Le crépuscule de Prométhée*, p. 235.
13 F. A. Hayek, *The Road to Serfdom*, p. 18.
14 Hayek, *The Road to Serfdom*, p. 18.
15 Hayek, *The Road to Serfdom*, p. 36.

16 Hayek, *The Road to Serfdom*, p. 92.
17 F. A. Hayek, *Law, Legislation and Liberty: A New Statement of the Liberal Principles of Justice and Equality*, vol. 2 (London: Routledge, 2012), p. 112.
18 B. Barber, 'Patriotism, autonomy and subversion', *Salmagundi*, 170–1 (2011), p. 125.
19 Flahault, *Le Crépuscule de Prométhée*, p. 247.
20 *Le Monde diplomatique*, April 2010.
21 E. Burke, *Reflections on the Revolution in France* (1790), available at http://www.constitution.org/eb/rev_fran.htm, accessed 27 March 2014.
22 Montesquieu, *The Persian Letters*, tr. J. Davidson, no. 105, available at http://en.wikisource.org/wiki/Persian_Letters/Letter_105, accessed 27 March 2014.
23 H. D. Lacordaire, *La Liberté de la parole évangélique* (Paris: Éditions du Cerf, 1996), pp. 342–3.
24 Cf. F. Flahault, *Le Paradoxe de Robinson* (Paris: Mille et une nuits, 2005).
25 A. Supiot, *Homo juridicus* (Paris: Le Seuil, 2005), p. 8.
26 Pascal, *Pensées*, 479 and 471.
27 Rousseau, *Émile*, available at http://www.gutenberg.org/cache/epub/5427/pg5427.html, accessed 27 March 2014; *Dialogues*, II, in *Oeuvres complètes* (Paris: Gallimard, 'Pléiade', 1959), vol. I, p. 810.
28 Montaigne, *Essays*, I, 28.
29 B. Constant, *De la liberté chez les Modernes* (Paris: LGF, 1980), p. 506; *Adolphe*, tr. Leonard Tancock (London: Penguin, 1980), p. 120, tr. modified.
30 B. Constant, *De la religion* (Arles: Actes Sud, 1999), p. 83; *Filangieri*, p. 135; *Diary* of 26 April 1805, in *Oeuvres* (Paris: Gallimard, 'Pléiade', 1979).
31 B. Constant, letter to Annette de Gérando, 5 June 1815, in B. Constant and Mme Récamier, *Lettres 1807–1830* (Paris: Champion, 1992).

Chapter 5 The Effects of Neoliberalism

1 Supiot, *Homo juridicus*, p. 9. I am here following his analysis.
2 B. Mika, *Die Feigheit der Frauen* (Munich: Bertelsmann, 2011), quoted in *Books*, 22 (2011), p. 11.
3 I am here drawing partly on J.-P. Le Goff. Cf. for example *La Barbarie douce* (Paris: La Découverte, 2003).
4 M. B. Crawford, *Shop Class as Soulcraft: An Inquiry into the Value of Work* (London: Penguin, 2009).
5 Supiot, *Homo juridicus*, pp. 255–6.
6 Supiot, *Homo juridicus*, p. 252.
7 I have devoted a section of my *The Fear of Barbarians* to this 'affair'.
8 V. Grossman, *Oeuvres* (Paris: Robert Laffont, 2006), p. 1011.
9 B. Constant, 'Préface' to *Mélanges de littérature et politique* (1829), in *De la liberté*, p. 519.

Chapter 6 Populism and Xenophobia

1 *Le Monde*, 20 November 2009.
2 Condorcet, *Cinq mémoires*, p. 91.
3 I have analysed this in detail in *The Fear of Barbarians*.
4 *Le Monde*, 10 May 2011.

Chapter 7 The Future of Democracy

1 Constant, *Diary*, 2 May 1804, in *Oeuvres*.
2 G. L. Mosse, *Toward the Final Solution: A History of European Racism* (New York: Howard Fertig, 1978; Harper & Row, 1980), pp. xiv–xv and 234.

3 R. Gary, *Tulipe* (Paris: Gallimard, 1970), p. 85; *La Bonne Moitié* (Paris: Gallimard, 1979), p. 141.
4 Cf. N. Huston, *Professeurs de désespoir* (Arles: Actes Sud, 2004), pp. 19–20.
5 Flahault, *Le Crépuscule de Prométhée*, pp. 285–6.

Index

197